The Unsung Heroics of Filipina Resistance

Fighters During the Pacific War

Pacific Atrocities Education

1945: 22-year-old Filipina who fought guerrilla forces in the Tarlac area of Luzon, poses with her gun, her cartridge belt and the Tarlac flag.[1]

---

[1] QRST, "1945 Headline Newspaper Women Guerrillas Fight in World War II," Ebay, Last Accessed July 8th, 2017, http://www.ebay.com/itm/1945-headline-newspaper-WOMEN-GUERRILLA-s-FIGHT-in-WW-II-FRANCE-PHILIPPINES-/371991116955?hash=item569c65fc9b.

Pinay Guerrilleras:
The Unsung Heroics of Filipina Resistance Fighters During the Pacific War

Author:
Stacey Anne Baterina Salinas

Researchers:
Jack Gray
Jack Demlow

Editors:
Nicholas A. Garcia
Jenny Chan

For information, address
Pacific Atrocities Education,
730 Commercial Street, San Francisco, CA 94108

ISBN: 978-1-947766-07-5

Acknowledgements

Writing a history about extraordinary heroines is no ordinary feat. Researching women's wartime experiences and contributions is unmistakably a tall order. Thoroughly covering Filipina guerrilla history required knowledge of the historiographies of various fields, including World War II, women's, American, Asian American, immigration, Philippines', and Pacific history. As a scholar of Asian American and American women's history, I had to incorporate the vastness of knowledge this book required to do justice to the heroes of the Pacific Theater, which required the time and energy of other patient and helpful hands. I would like to thank Jack Gray for his correspondence, research, and brilliant notes on MacArthur's Pacific Campaign. Outlining military history is a tedious task, particularly for a social historian such as myself. Thus, I am grateful for Pacific Atrocities Education's (PAE) know-how, and keen instincts in assigning me such a great team to accomplish this work. On that note, I would like to thank the co-founder of PAE, Jenny Chan, for allowing me to continue my research and explore my passion for Filipino American women's history. Being able to find such a supporting, inviting, and a warm institution of scholars, educators, and activists has been such a blessing these past two years. As well, I would like to acknowledge Nicholas Garcia, who spent hours diligently line-editing my sometimes jumbled words, which I personally would not have been able to find time for as I juggled graduate school, work, and everything in between this past year. Thank you for helping me to find my voice from the various outlines, drafts, and lagging Google documents that this piece eventually transformed from.

Of course, I would also like to humbly acknowledge those who encouraged me behind the scenes during my writing and researching process. I would not have the ability, determination, or mental toughness to pursue such a strenuous academic endeavor without the support of my family and mentors. This work, the culmination of those endless nights surrounded by books and computer screens, exists because of my family, who instilled in me my cultural heritage, and because of my mentors, James Papp, Kyu H. Kim, Robyn Rodriguez, and Kathleen Cairns, who told me to keep on trekking.

Thank you also to the Aremas and Poblete families, who were kind enough to share with me their painful experiences of the war. Listening to their first-hand accounts, being able to ask questions, and reliving with them as to how the war transformed their lives, allowed me the rare opportunity to step back in time. This work ultimately aims to honor the women whose lives and sacrifices dot the pages of this book. For without their tireless dedication to country, family, and freedom, the world would not know of the honor and strength attached to the meaning of being Filipina.

About the Author

Stacey Anne Baterina Salinas is a history Ph.D. student currently attending the University of California, Davis. She received her Bachelor's degree from the University of California, Irvine and her Master's degree from California Polytechnic State University, San Luis Obispo, both in American History. Her research focus is on Asian American History, centering on the roles of Asian American women and their impact on America's Civil Rights Movement(s) and contributions to the diversity of American women's experience. She dedicates her late nights of research and writing to the many men and women who fought for her grandparents' and parents' native homes in the Philippines. Her maternal grandfather served as a Filipino USAFFE soldier, drafted from Baguio City, and survived the Bataan Death March. His history, along with her paternal grandmother's late night tales of her terrifying confrontations with the Japanese as a young girl in the northern provinces of Luzon, serve as proof of the impacts and legacies of Asian America. Their stories and perseverance helped fuel her desire to write histories on the humble heroes and innocents unable to give voice to their struggles, wisdom, and experiences.

Table of Contents

Acknowledgements _____ 7

About the Author _____ 11

Introduction _____ 15

Chapter 1
The Japanese Occupation of the Philippine
Islands: Pinays Answering the Call to Arms _____ 25

Chapter 2
The Hearts of the Huk: The Fierce *Heneralas*
and *Kumanders* of the Hukbalahap Guerrillas ___ 41

Chapter 3
The Glamorous *Guerrilleras*: Amazons of the
Pacific Theater_____ 67

Chapter 4
Filipina American Veterans: Recovering the
Extraordinary Feats of the Ordinary Pinays _____ 99

Chapter 5
The Legacy of the Asian Woman Soldier _____ 129

Conclusion_____ 145

Works Cited _____ 154

Introduction

The Philippines has a remarkable history of tenacious, ardent, and fiery female warriors. Filipino women, Filipinas, have demonstrated their cultural pride and admiration for their ancestral homeland through their military prowess and leadership. As early as the medieval period, Filipina warriors like Princess Urduja commanded armies, negotiated Pacific trade, managed tribal alliances, and shaped earlier notions of Philippine femininity and culture. She challenged the patriarchal gender norms practiced by her contemporary southeast Asian rivals.

While traveling to Southeast Asia, the famous Muslim scholar and explorer Ibn Battuta recorded that the northern island of the Philippines—known previously as the land of Tawalisi prior to the era of Spanish colonialism—was single-handedly controlled by the multilingual warrior princess.[1] Her military prowess and

---

[1] Davis Waines, *The Odyssey of Ibn Battuta: Uncommon Tales of a Medieval Adventurer* (New York: I.B. Tauris & Co, 2010), "Epilogue."

Artwork by artist Macabuhay depicting the Philippine medieval warrior princess Urduja, circa 1940.[2]

at combat were remarkable. Confident in her abilities, Urduja proclaimed that she would only marry a man brave and skilled enough to defeat her in hand to hand

---

[2] Ligaya, "Princess Urduja: Folk Hero's/Heroines from the Philippines," Last Modified 28th, 2012, Last Accessed August 24th, 2018, http://pinoy-culture.tumblr.com/post/26084878583/princess-urduja-folk-herosheroines-from-the.

combat.[3] Her armies included both men and women. Her ministers and advising consul were comprised of female elders. She commanded military expeditions throughout the coast and provinces of Pangasinan on the island of Luzon. News of her military exploits and growing empire traveled as far as India, China, and Malaysia.[4] Oral histories depict Urduja as the quintessential Filipina Amazon, and indeed, her martial victories continue to be passed down in traditional Philippine, Chinese, and Southeast Asian folklore.

There are other Filipinas as remarkable as Princess Urduja. These include the women who led and fought within major sects of guerrilla resistance against Spanish colonialism in the eighteenth to nineteenth centuries. One of the most famous and influential of these nationalist resistance leaders was Gabriela Silang (1723-1763). After Filipino Spanish loyalists killed her husband, Silang assumed control of his guerrilla units in Ilocos Sur. She is traditionally depicted as fighting alongside her countrymen on the front lines, leading the liberation of towns and barrios of the Ilocos region. Silang was more successful than her male nationalist contemporaries, leading colonial Spanish authorities to consider her the gravest threat to their occupation of the Philippines. The villagers and city folk

---

[3] Antonio Del Castillo y Tuazon, *Princess Urduja, Queen of the Orient Seas: Before and After her Time in the Political Orbit of the Shri-vi-ja-ya and the Madjapahit Maritime Empire: a Pre-Hispanic HIstory of the Philippines* (University of Michigan, 1998), 51-64.

[4] Waines, *The Odyssey of Ibn Battuta*, "Epilogue."

of Northern Luzon even gave her the honorary title of *henerala*, meaning woman general.[5]

Silang was eventually captured and executed by the Spanish, but not before she dealt major blows to their infantry and confidence as a colonial empire. As such, even after her death, Silang would continue to hold an elevated position in Filipino oral histories and folklore. In both Philippine feminist and patriotic artwork, Silang is often depicted holding a traditional longsword, or bolo, while on horseback. Because of her fortitude and courage in battle, Silang is celebrated as a Philippine heroine, patriot, and proto-feminist, who planted the early seeds of colonial resistance and Philippine nationalism.

The centuries-long Spanish occupation of the Philippines bred other Filipino groups like Silang's, groups that aggressively advocated for Philippine independence. One of these early groups was the Katipunan. Formed in 1892, the Katipunan allowed for the recruitment of women into their ranks. The efforts of female combatants during this period of Philippine resistance have been mostly overlooked, with the focus being more on the women working behind the scenes in supporting roles (couriers, nurses, supportive wives, and homemakers who fed and housed the guerrilla troops).

But this is starting to change. In more recent histories, narratives of Filipinas donning crucial military

---

[5] Alicia Arrizon, *Queering Mestizaje: Transculturation and Performance* (Ann Arbor: University of Michigan Press, 2009), 137.

roles for the Katipunan movement have surfaced. Gregoria de Jesus, the wife of the founding member of the Katipunan, Andres Bonifacio, was the first female member of the Katipunan. Gregoria accompanied her husband to the male-dominated meetings of the Katipunan, and fought in the guerrilla army against the Spanish and Filipino loyalists under the name of Manuela Gonzaga.[6] As a *guerrillera*, Gregoria also served as the Katipunan's Custodian of Records, and was responsible for keeping the organization's documents and funds in order.[7] When captured by a rival sect of the Katipunan, Gregoria was tied to a tree, threatened with beatings by male soldiers, and robbed of her valuable possessions—including her wedding ring. She was then savagely raped by Colonel Agapito Bonzon.[8] Even so, Gregoria refused to divulge the whereabouts of Katipunan leaders and their funds.

As vice president of the female charter of the Katipunan, and as a soldier, Gregoria—like so many other unsung guerrilla heroes—advocated for Philippine nationalism and independence and thus was more than just a supporting character in the grander narra-

---

[6] Robert H. Boyer, *Sundays in Manila* (Quezon City: The University of the Philippines Press, 2010), 136.

[7] Ligaya Caballes, "10 Kickass Pilipina Warriors that You Probably Never Heard of," *Pinoy Culture.com: Your Source for Everything Pilipino*, Last Modified August 28th, 2014, Last Accessed August 23rd, 2018, http://pinoy-culture.com/10-kickass-pilipina-warriors-in-history-that-you-probably-never-heard-of/.

[8] Cecilio D. Duka, *Struggle for Freedom* (Manila: Rex Publishing, 2008), 150-152.

tive of the Philippine Revolt.[9] And, above all else, because Gregoria preserved the Katipunan's records, we not only know more about its mission and the nationalist rhetoric it employed, but we also have access to the legacies of Filipina wartime activism that otherwise would have been lost.[10]

Another Filipina guerrilla fighter, or *guerrillera*, whose valor serves as a testament of Southeast Asian women's political activism and military leadership during the colonial era, is Agueda Kahabagan. Agueda Kahabagan is the only Filipina to earn the title of general in the Army of the Philippine Republic.[11] Unfortunately, we know little of Agueda's life before and after the Philippine revolt. What we do know is that Agueda was appointed by Philippine national hero, General Emilio Aguinaldo, to lead all-male units against both Spanish and American troops at the turn

---

[9] The Katipunan's "female charter" was essentially a female-run version of the larger organization. Historically, Filipino movements tend to work this way, with female factions splintering from male-led central organizations. While these female factions share essentially the same goals as their male counterparts, they often have their own unique identities. Florentine Rodao and Felice Noelle Rodriguez ed. *The Philippine Revolution of 1896: Ordinary Lives in Extraordinary Times* (Manila: Ateneo de Manila University Press, 2001), 17, 18.

[10] National Centennial Commission, *Sulong Pilipina! Sulong Pilipinas!: A Compilation of Filipino Women Centennial Awardees* (National Centennial Commission, Women Sector, 1999), 390-400.

[11] Beatrice Celdran, "I Am... Woman: Historic Filipinas," *Philippine Tatler*, Last Modified August 7th, 2014, Last Accessed August 23rd, 2018, https://ph.asiatatler.com/life/i-am-woman.

of the nineteenth century.[12] Like other Filipina Amazon-type warriors and *guerrilleras*, she is often depicted as a long-haired soldier on horseback, armed with a dagger and rifle. Known to wear white into battle, her compatriots gave her the nickname "Joan of Arc of the Tagalogs."[13]

After the Spanish-American War, a new generation of *guerrilleras* continued the fight against American colonization. American propaganda claimed that they were in the Philippines to aid their "brown brothers" by teaching them democracy and nurturing their potential for self-determination.[14] In reality, the Americans merely sought to import cheap Philippine labor to fuel their growing agricultural industries in Hawaii and the American Pacific Northwest. To this end, American businesses exploited the islands' natural resources. Furthermore, the American protectorate system continued to oversee and take advantage of Spain's colonial-semi-feudal land system, offering major seats of power to rich landowners, leaving most of the population at a bare subsistence level.[15]

---

[12] Caballes, "10 Kickass Pilipina Warriors that You Probably Never Heard of," *Pinoy Culture.com: Your Source for Everything Pilipino*, Last Modified August 28th, 2014, Last Accessed August 23rd, 2018, http://pinoy-culture.com/10-kickass-pilipina-warriors-in-history-that-you-probably-never-heard-of/.

[13] D.J. Walker, *Spanish Women and the Colonial Wars* (Baton Rouge: Louisiana State University Press, May 2008), 13, 14.

[14] Kevin L. Nadal, *Filipino American Psychology: A Handbook of Theory, Research, and Clinical Practice* (Bloomington: Authorhouse, 2009), 94.

[15] Peter A. Poole, *Politics and Society in Southeast Asia* (North Carolina: McFarland & Company, 2009), 159, 160.

In response to American and Philippine elites' mismanagement and profiteering during the early twentieth century, the Sakdalista Movement, founded by Benigno Ramos in 1930, advocated for immediate Philippine independence as well as estate redistribution. Salud Algabre, another Filipina *guerrillera*, directed several operations during the 1930s Sakdalista Movement, and was the only female Sakdalista military recruit to achieve the title of general.[16]

The Japanese occupation of the Philippine Islands mirrored earlier efforts by Spain and the United States, in that they attempted to exact absolute control over Filipino culture, government, trade, labor, natural resources, and peoples. The liberation of the Philippines from the Japanese Imperial Army, like the past revolts against Spanish and American regimes, required the combined efforts of men and women from all walks of life. As with our previous examples, the efforts of the women who contributed to the war effort against the Japanese have largely been ignored. Indeed, Filipinas have either been highlighted for the supporting roles they played, or more often than not, as helpless victims. The erasure of women's contributions to these resistance efforts perpetuates the notion that war, military, and state formation are territories

---

[16] John Witeck, "Introduction," as found in *Navigating Islands and Continents: Conversations and Contestations in and Around the Pacific, Selected Essays Vol. 17* (Honolulu: College of Languages, Linguistics and Literature University of Hawai'i and the East West Center, 2000) ed. Cynthia Franklin, Ruth Hsu, Suzanne Kosanke, 8.

exclusive to men. On the contrary, we have seen how women of color like Urduja, Agueda, and Gregoria served as soldiers and military leaders, demonstrating the extent to which the creation of an independent Philippine state required the participation of women to succeed.

The Philippine revolts at the turn of the nineteenth century—and well into the first half of the twentieth century—represent major stages where Filipinas demonstrated their nationalist and political fervor. The invasion of the Philippine Islands in January of 1942 served as yet another hurdle in the road towards Philippine independence. But as with previous colonial invasions, Filipina *guerrilleras* heeded the call to defend their lands from yet another oppressive imperial occupation.

Above all else, this book is a testament to the experiences, struggles, and contributions of the Filipina women who fought for Philippine independence in the Pacific Theater. Without their steadfastness, selflessness, and courage to protect their loved ones, home, and country, the liberation of the Philippines would have failed, and MacArthur, along with the rest of the United States Armed Forces of the Far East (USAFFE), would not have been able to regain their foothold in the Pacific.

Chapter 1

The Japanese Occupation of the Philippine Islands: Pinays Answering the Call to Arms

The invasion of the Philippines was the culmination of many years of Japanese expansion throughout the Pacific and greater East Asia. The Japanese sphere of influence extended over Korea, Formosa (Taiwan), Manchuria, and Inner Mongolia by the 1930s.[1] Their imperial expansion throughout East and Southeast Asia proved that its economy could support a military on par with even its western rivals' militaries. As Japan began encroaching upon Western colonial territories in the Pacific, American President Franklin Delano Roosevelt's concerns regarding Japan's expansive imperial presence in the Pacific grew. On December 7th, 1941, tensions boiled over. Japan's attack on Pearl Harbor, coupled with their earlier invasions of East

---

[1]Masato Kimura, Tosh Minohara ed. *Tumultuous Decade: Empire, Society, and Diplomacy in 1930s Japan* (Toronto: University of Toronto Press, 2013), 103, 130, 200, 252.

Asia, and entry into Southeast Asia in 1942, reflected their imperialist attempt to create a Pan-Asian state. For both the United States and Japan, the Philippines was a contentious space to these rivaling imperialist powers. Japan understood the value of the Philippines' ports and natural resources as a strategic advantage in expanding their imperial presence in Southeast Asia. Furthermore, by folding the Philippine archipelago into Japan's Pan-Asia model, the Imperial Japanese Army could eliminate western intrusions and major American military strongholds in the Pacific.

Prior to the attack on Pearl Harbor, the Commonwealth of the Philippines was largely shaped by American colonial interests and policies. The Jones Act of 1916 formed a Philippine legislature guided by a newly drafted constitution, establishing the basis for a transitional government overseen by American policymakers intent on supposedly establishing a foundation for Philippine democracy.[2] The trend of American hands politicking Philippine domestic policies and relations would ultimately translate in the following decades into the 1935 Tydings-McDuffie Act. This act defined the Philippines as en route to becoming a full-fledged democratic and sovereign state under "American benevolence and tutelage," which would be guaranteed

---

[2] Neil A. Wynn, *Historical Dictionary from the Great War to the Great Depression* (Lanham: Scarecrow Press, 2014), 186.

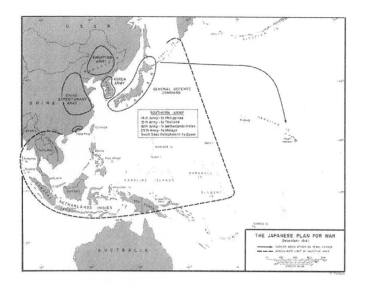

Japanese Military Strategy in the Pacific 1941-1942.[3]

total independence by 1945.[4] By 1941, however, the United States continued to retain significant control over the islands, especially with regard to its military, as well as maintained a strong naval presence throughout the main ports of the archipelago.

For Imperial Japan, the invasion of the Philippines pushed them closer towards their goal of creating and leading a pan-Asian empire. It also allowed them to oust their Western rivals, who had, within the last decade, refused to conduct further trade with them via

---

[3] Louis Morton, *United States Army in World War II: The War in the Pacific, Strategy & Command: The First Two Years* (Office of the Chief of Military History, Department of the Army, 1962), 106.

[4] Bill Ong Hing, *Making and Remaking Asian America Through Immigration Policy: 1850-1990* (Stanford: Stanford University Press, 1993), 35.

FDR's Export Control Act of 1940.[5] Such embargo acts, and the West's intervention in foreign relations concerning Japan's expansion and imperial gains in China, Korea, and Formosa (Taiwan), significantly curtailed Japan's aims of building an imperialist empire to rival both America and European nations. Because they housed American military bases within close proximity to Japan, the Philippines were among the first priorities for invasion in the Pacific Theater. Immediately after the surrender of the Philippine Armed Forces, the Imperial Japanese Army committed the first of many atrocities that would characterize their wartime occupation of the Philippines.

The Bataan Death March, as it came to be called, resulted in the deaths of thousands of Filipinos and Americans. The march stretched to roughly a sixty--three-mile trek on foot.[6] Forced to walk without food or water, and under constant threat of torture or death, Filipino and American soldiers who survived the march would continue to experience brutality, slave labor, and starvation within Japanese manned Prisoner of War camps. Other survivors were forced

---

[5] The Export Control Act of 1940 was authorized the President, in the interest of national defense, to prohibit or curtail the export of basic war materials. Under that act, licenses were refused for the export to Japan of aviation gasoline and most types of machine tools, beginning in August 1940. Erik J. Dahl, *Intelligence and Surprise Attack: Failure and Success from Pearl Harbor to 9/11 and Beyond* (Georgetown University Press, 2013), 43.

[6] Robert Greenberger, *Snapshots in History: The Bataan Death March: World War II in the Pacific* (Mankato: Compass Point Books, 2009), 32.

to work on "hell ships," where they were used as manual laborers throughout the Pacific Theater and left vulnerable to attacks by their own Navy.[7]

The Japanese occupation of the Philippines lasted for over two years. While the Allies reconvened and fought their way across the Pacific, the Philippine peoples began a ferocious underground resistance movement. Japanese brutality, combined with a lack of food and medical supplies, meant that the underground resistance required all available hands and voices to lend themselves to the cause of liberating the Philippines. Guerilla fighters ambushed Japanese patrols, sabotaged weapon production efforts in local factories, and secretly gave information to U.S. forces via radio and off-the-coast meetings.[8] The resistance movement prevented the Imperial Japanese Army from establishing total control over the islands by disrupting their lines of communication, pushing back their forces into more open and vulnerable terrain, and pilfering their warehouses of ammunition and supplies.

But such effective and stalwart guerrilla subterfuge was doubly met by the Imperial Japanese Army's bru-

---

[7] Raymond Laymont-Brown, *Ships from Hell: Japanese War Crimes on the High Seas* (Stroud: Sutton Publishing, 2002). Tom Bennett, *World War II Wrecks of the Philippines: WWII Shipwrecks of the Philippines* (Happy Fish Publications, 2010), 27.

[8] Travis Ingham, *Rendezvous By Submarine: The Story of Charles Parsons and the Guerrilla-Soldiers in the Philippines* (Los Angeles: The Bowsprit Press, 2018), 106.

tal treatment of guerrillas, guerrilla sympathizers, and local civilians. Testimonies and first-hand accounts of the Japanese occupation given during the War Crimes Trials following the war are filled with stories of pillage, rape, and murder of noncombatants of all ages.[9]

War Department, Public Relations Office
Bruna R. Calvan and Carmen Lanot (left and center) with Guedelia M. Pablan, M.D. (right) cared for Filipinos and Americans at Hermosa on Bataan throughout the occupation.

The Filipina led medical unit of Bataan, circa 1945.[10]

---

[9] Timothy P. Maga, *Judgement at Tokyo: The Japanese War Crimes Trials* (Lexington: University of Press of Kentucky, 2001), xi, 67, 108.

[10] A snippet of the Bataan medical unit captioned, "Dr. Pablan and her staff after they had returned from the fish ponds to Hermosa where they reopened their hospital when the Americans arrived." Source: May 1945 issue of the American Journal of Nursing. "The 10 Most Incredible Filipina Warriors of World War II," *FilipiKnow.Net*, Last Modified December 5th, 2018, Last Accessed December 19th, 2018, https://filipiknow.net/filipina-heroes-of-wwii/.

Civilians were killed or beaten for information, and those who were suspected resistance fighters or sympathizers were kidnapped, tortured, and killed without sufficient evidence or proper trials.[11]

Women, who were especially vulnerable to the Japanese occupiers, risked their safety to support the resistance. Local women were kidnapped and turned into sex laborers, forced to serve the imperial army as "comfort women."[12] Filipina women faced the combined threats of rape, kidnap, torture, and murder. And yet, *pinay guerrilleras* forged ahead despite these insurmountable odds.

Instances of Filipina wartime resilience and bravery, although rarely recorded, can be found through various Philippine and Filipino-American newspapers and journals during and after the war. For instance, the American Journal of Nursing in 1945 provided a short tribute to Filipina nurses, Bruna R. Calvan and Carmen Lanot, and *pinay* doctor, Guedelia M. Pablan. These Bataan medical professionals saw firsthand the grim and cruel treatment of both American and Filipino soldiers during the Death March. The three continued to stay in Bataan, even after the Japanese defeated MacArthur and secured the Philippines, in order to continue to heal and protect wounded civilians

---

[11] Toshiyuki Tanaka, *Hidden Horrors: Japanese War Crimes in World War II* (Westview Press, 1996), 21-26, 32.

[12] Margaret D. Stetz, Bonnie B. C. Oh ed., *Legacies of the Comfort Women of World War II* (New York: Routledge, 2015), 75.

and soldiers in hiding. They did this despite the ongoing threat of Japanese military violence. After their hospital was burned down by Japanese troops, they moved to a convent to continue their work. That convent was also destroyed, causing the Filipina led medical crew to make their own makeshift health center by nearby fishing ponds, where they continued to aide in the recovery of malaria afflicted guerrilla troops by forging paperwork for more orders of quinine, which they sent to afflicted soldiers in the mountain camps via canoe across Manila Bay.[13]

With barely enough food and rations to sustain their own wellbeing, Dr. Pablan and her small cohort of dedicated nurses survived the war, and restored the health and stamina of the resistance. Their bravery and dedication to their profession and the Philippine peoples would be recognized after the war. Both Philippine and American nurses who stayed to heal the wounded and sick on Bataan were given the title as the "Angels of Bataan & Corregidor."[14]

The Bataan Angels made the best of a desperate situation. Japanese occupation placed civilians in constant danger and deprived them of their basic rights

---

[13] Sergeant Karl Ritt, "Filipino Nurses on Bataan," *American Journal of Nursing*, Vol. 45 No. 5 (May 1945), 346-347.

[14]The Pre-Medical Society of the Ateneo, "Filipina Angels of Bataan," *The Pre-Medical Society of the Ateneo*, Last Modified April 9th, 2015, Last Accessed December 27th, 2018, https://www.facebook.com/the.pmsa/photos/a.146528742097296/810066542410176/?type=1&theater.

and liberties. The IJA also made life difficult for anybody who, like the Angels, sympathized with the Allies, as Japanese officers were specifically tasked with stamping them out. This, combined, with the lack of trained military hands to combat Imperial Japanese troops, made the contribution of women an essential addition and asset to the underground resistance.

A plaque made in honor of the Philippine and American nurses stationed at Bataan that can be found at the General Wainwright and Nurses Memorial on Corregidor.[15]

---

[15] Karl Welteke, "Corregidor-Then and Now: 503rd PRCT Heritage Battalion, The Fall of the Philippines, Battle of Manila," *Corregidorproboards.com*, Last Modified August 3rd, 2015, Last Accessed December 22nd, 2018, http://corregidor.proboards.com/thread/1848/generalwainwright.

Absence of the Filipina Resistance Fighter: Filling the Gaps of Women's World History

War is a hyper-masculine arena that emphasizes the actions of men. Indeed, American World War II histories, in particular, tend to highlight the victories of valorous male soldiers abroad, idolize the distinguished generals who commanded them, and memorialize the steadfast presidents who used noble democratic rhetoric to steer their countries towards world peace. As popular and mainstream historical narratives regarding the buildup of the Pacific War demonstrate, the main actors of the war typically referenced include MacArthur, Franklin D. Roosevelt, and Nimitz. They are discussed alongside a handful of influential military leaders of Asian descent—primarily high ranking members of the Imperial Japanese Army—like Toyoda, Koga, and Yamamoto. What this means is that most other actors, despite the significance of their actions, are left out of the World War II narrative. This includes the women discussed here, who, unfortunately, have tended to fall between the cracks of history.

American women during both world wars are depicted as demonstrating their patriotism through supportive roles as humble sisters and homemakers. American women fulfilled these supportive roles by rallying for war bonds and food drives and rationing meals and canned goods in honor of troops abroad. One of America's most celebrated icons is that of the wartime female patriot: the hard-as-nails defense industry worker, Rosie the Riveter, brought to life most famously by the artwork of Norman Rockwell and J. Howard Miller. In the United States, World War II provided the economic gateway for women to branch out of the domestic sphere and work for higher wages as clerks, secretaries, or other positions typically associated with women who labored outside of the home. Those who did not work in the shipyards and smelting industries supported the war effort abroad as Red Cross nurses, pilots, entertainers for the troops, or even as spies working within pocket resistance movements in the Pacific or European fronts. Examples include Margaret Utinsky and Claire Philipps, who provided supplies and intelligence to the surviving POWs of Bataan and local Filipino *guerrillas*.[16]

Like American women, Filipinas also challenged gender expectations under the duress of extreme wartime by taking on active military roles, proving that they too were exceptional patriots and fighters. While Filipino women in the occupied Philippines faced the constant threat of sexual harassment from Japanese soldiers, they were less likely to be arrested as spies or guerillas, as these were roles the Japanese typically

---

[16] Theresa Kaminski, *Angels of the Underground: The American Women Who Resisted the Japanese in World War II* (New York: Oxford University Press, 2016), ix, 200, 401.

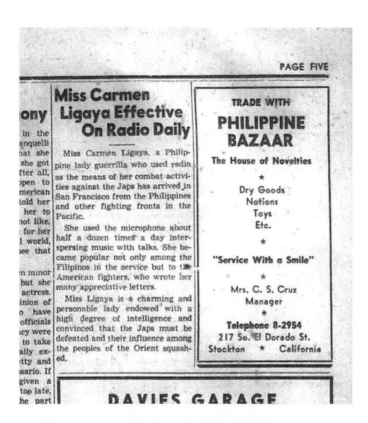

Short snippet in *The Philippines Mail* on the "lady guerrilla, Carmen Ligaya, who used the radio to provide intelligence information to the Filipino resistance, and liberation morale to both Filipino and American Allied soldiers, circa 1945.[17]

associated with men. Such gendered assumptions allowed women more freedom to travel between villages, without the overly heavy suspicions of Japanese

---

[17] The Philippines Mail Staff Writer, "Miss Carmen Ligaya Effective On Radio Daily," *The Philippines Mail*, January 1945, Steinbeck Public Library, Salinas.

soldiers, who expected subversive activity from the male rather than female civilians.[18] Traditional perceptions of war as a male occupied zone made women ideal operatives for a broad range of guerilla activities. Women were excellent intelligence agents, as they could get far closer to enemy-occupied territory than male guerillas. They also acted as liaisons between guerilla camps and civilian villages, where they monitored the safety and communication lines of villages that supported the resistance.[19]

Celia Mariano Pomeroy is one such *guerrillera* whose liaison and courier work was central to the resistance. Among her other self-assigned *guerrillera* duties, Pomeroy inspired and instructed local villagers and guerrillas, showing them how to organize and network while simultaneously rallying villages with rhetoric emphasizing liberation and democracy. She later became the editor of a resistance newspaper, *Katubusan ng Bayan,* or *Redemption of the Nation.* She also was made the educational secretary of the central Luzon Bureau.[20] Pomeroy would come into frequent contact with the Japanese as she traveled between vil-

[18] Vina A. Lanzona, *Amazons of the Huk Rebellion: Gender, Sex, and Revolution in the Philippines* (Madison: University of Wisconsin Press, 2009, 55.

[19] Lanzona, *Amazons of the Huk Rebellion, 60.*

[20] Jim Richardson, "Celia Mariano Pomeroy: Communist Revolutionary Who Went on to Teach in London Primary Schools," *Independent Minds,* Last Modified October 22, 2009, Last Accessed December 18th, 2018, https://www.independent.co.uk/news/obituaries/celia-mariano-pomeroy-communist-revolutionary-who-went-on-to-teach-in-london-primary-schools-1806786.html.

lages. She survived numerous ambushes and attacks while under close Japanese surveillance and was deemed a priority target by Japanese soldiers tasked with ferreting out Filipino guerrillas.[21] With her close relations and networking with local villagers, Pomeroy was able to remain safe and concealed on her missions from the IJA.

Female guerrillas like Pomeroy were crucial in spreading Allied propaganda and connecting other guerrilla units to USAFFE intelligence. The resistance's courier system thus was highly effective primarily because women guerrillas took advantage of Japan's underestimation of women's capabilities in war. Using gendered expectations to their advantage, Filipina guerrillas feigned vulnerability to acquire a strategic edge, catching the Japanese off-guard. In so doing, Filipina guerrillas became invaluable assets on the frontline of the resistance effort, working tirelessly to maintain open communications, establish networks, boost morale, and ensure the overall security of both the resistance movement and Filipino civilians.

Working as female operatives within the guerrilla resistance required both mental and physical toughness. *Pinay* guerrilleras navigated male-dominated military zones where women were expected to conform to culturally entrenched gender conventions. Indeed, not only did they have to deal with their male

---

21 Lanzona, *Amazons of the Huk Rebellion*, 148-153.

peers within the male-dominated Filipino resistance effort, but they also had to risk their lives infiltrating the violent and unpredictable areas occupied by Japanese imperial authorities and their Filipinos allies (known as the *makapili*). In these occupied regions, a unique brand of hyper-masculine "machismo" reigned supreme, forcing some *pinay* guerrilleras to not act fully on their liberal patriotic inclinations, and instead, forced them to conform more towards traditional standards of Filipina femininity if they wished to participate in the resistance. Despite these gendered setbacks, *pinay* guerrilleras held their own and were crucial to building the foundation of the resistance through their efforts as fighters, spies, organizers, and medical personnel. *Guerrilleras* formed their own standard of patriot, soldier, and woman—a standard that intricately blended traditional gender norms and challenged machismo perceptions of female agency.

Chapter 2

The Hearts of the Huk: The Fierce *Heneralas* and *Kumanders* of the Hukbalahap Guerrillas

The only surviving artistic rendition of the Huk *Kapampangan* commander, *Kumander Mameng* aka Elena Poblete, Kumander Mameng of Minalin. She led her own unit and fought on the front lines. Her legacy as a war hero can only be found in two surviving verified sources: one written by Moises Lopez, a foot soldier who served in Poblete's squadron, and the other by the famous Huk commander Simeona Punsalan, who kept accounts detailing her time with Kumander Mameng, whom she considered a friend.[1]

---

[1] FilipiKnow.net, "The 10 Most Incredible Filipina Warriors of World War II," *FilipiKnow*, Last Modified 2018, Last Accessed December 17th, 2018, https://filipiknow.net/filipina-heroes-of-wwii/#2_Elena_Poblete. Photo Credit, Joseph Dado, the Juan D. Nepomuceno Center for Kapampangan Studies of Holy Angel University.

The underground resistance during the Japanese occupation was composed of various organizations and units. Although all branches sought to liberate the Philippine islands from Imperial Japan, not all guerrilla groups shared similar philosophies on war or postwar goals centered on rebuilding a democratic state void of neo-colonial influences. Of the 277 officially recognized guerrilla units, the Hukbalahap was one of the most politically aggressive and motivated in their efforts towards liberation.[2] The Huk guerrillas threaded their resistance efforts with their left-leaning socialist rhetoric centered on achieving true sovereignty for the Philippines. In addition to anti-colonial sentiments, Huk praxis aimed to oust the Spanish and American socio-economic policy that enforced a semi-feudal land distribution system where wealthy landowners held control over the production of the majority of the nation's lands and therefore solely held the rights to the production of natural resources and manufacturing of domestic products, all at the expense of landless peasants and farmers who tilled the land for little pay and board.

The Hukbalahap began as a socialist organization composed of a diverse cast of laborers and grassroots activists; peasant farmers, workers' unions, communist

---

[2] Larry S. Schmidt, American Involvement in the Filipino Resistance Movement on Mindanao During the Japanese Occupation, 1942-1945, Master of Military Art and Science Thesis (U.S. Army Command and General Staff College, 1982), 2.

party members, and both urban and rural laborers. The founders and party members hailed from both the Socialist and Philippine Communist Party, and throughout the 1930s, prior to the Japanese occupation, served as active nationalists and revolutionaries who sought an independent communist Philippine state. The leader of the Philippines first official communist organization, the Worker's Party, was Crisanto Evangelista.[3] It was not until after the Japanese capture and executions of Evangelista and his head deputy, Abad Santos, that Evangelista's communist and socialist guerrillas unified in addressing themselves officially as the Hukbalahap in 1942.

The name of their resistance branch, Hukbalahap, translates to "people who are against the Japanese" or "the people's army against the Japanese," and resonated with local Filipino communities who experienced the abuse of the Japanese military presence.[4] Evangelista and his CPP guerrillas were depicted as bandits akin to Robin Hood, who helped the defenseless peasant folk by attacking Japanese military centers and redistributing the supplies they confiscated. The Huks were so successful in their raids and strategy that the

---

[3] Robert R. Smith, *The Hukbalahap Insurgency: Economic, Political and Military Factors*, (Washington, D.C.: Office of the Chief of Military History, 1963), 3-9.

[4] Major Lawrence M. Greenberg, *Historical Analysis Series: THE HUKBALAHAP INSURRECTION, A Case Study of a Successful, Anti-Insurgency Operation in the Philippines, 1946-1955* (Washington D.C.: U.S. Government Printing Office, 1986), 14.

Japanese gained very little control and terrain in most of Central Luzon, the main island of the Philippines.

The Huk rebellion against the Japanese was composed of two main branches, the guerillas themselves, who lived in camps in the forest and carried out operations against Japanese troops, and the BUDC (Barrio United Defense Corps), which were resistance groups based in the villages.[5] The BUDC operated as support units to the guerillas themselves. The BUDCs and their members would organize local support for the Huk rebellion, keep supplies and food out of Japanese hands and instead give them to the guerrillas, and perform all the functions of a local government. By involving locals and their respective barrio communities, and authorizing them control over their own resources, the Huks placed a great deal of trust and responsibility on their fellow countrymen to aid in the liberation movement.

The emphasis on laborer's rights, land redistribution, and the eventual creation of a more egalitarian state made the Huk movement popular amongst the peasant and working classes. Evangelista's political ideologies emphasized socialist and anti-colonial ideologies, which in turn allowed for a blurring of other traditional labor spheres. Thus, the Huk movement was open to women's labor and participation, which attracted many women to its cause.

---

[5] Edward Geary Lansdale, *In the Midst of Wars: An American's Mission to Southeast Asia* (New York: Fordham University Press, 1991), 7.

Originally, the Huks only intended to recruit men for their organization. The first women who joined their ranks were family members of its male recruits. As the war progressed, more women—whose family members were involved with the Huk resistance—decided to join voluntarily.[6] Male recruits were usually trained as foot soldiers or officers. Women, on the other hand, were relegated to support roles, such as secretarial, propaganda, or medical-related field work.[7] The vast majority of the Huk movement's female medical personnel worked as nurses. Filipinas treated overwhelming numbers of both local civilians and soldiers who suffered from malaria and injuries on the frontlines. Huk communist rhetoric, combined with the high demand for fighters, volunteers, and nurses, made the Huk resistance an opportune space for Filipinas to become directly involved with both spreading patriotic fervor and aiding rebel efforts throughout the duration of the war.

War gave Huk women the opportunity to take on important roles that once were deemed suitable only for men. Like most underground resistance militaries, the Huks were constantly short of resources, meaning they had to rely a great deal on Filipina labor to make up the difference. Large female support staffs meant

---

[6] Vina A. Lanzona, *Amazons of the Huk Rebellion: Gender, Sex, and Revolution in the Philippines* (Madison: University of Wisconsin Press, 2009), 40-43.

[7] Lanzona, *Amazons of the Huk Rebellion*, 52.

that more Filipino male guerrillas were available to serve in combat roles. Filipinas supported the underground resistance not only by providing medical care for male combatants, but, perhaps more importantly, by maintaining lines of communication and building networks of the barrio, village, and town support for the guerrilla cause.

Filipina Huks were tasked with winning over locals, convincing villagers and townspeople to defy the occupying Japanese troops, and, most importantly, to provide the basic necessities such as food, medical supplies, and temporary housing and cover for the guerrillas. Therefore, the critical efforts of Huk women—who provided the means for collecting the essentials for the Resistance—reveals the crucial role that female laborers played. Without the dedicated women operating as nurses, support staff, ralliers, and community contacts, the Huk resistance would not have gained enough momentum, and thus, would not have been as much of a threat to the Japanese occupation.

Felipa Culala of Candaba, *Kumander* Dayang Dayang

Artist Dos Garcia's rendition of Commander
Felipa Culala, aka Dayang-Dayang.[8]

Felipa Culala was a female Huk leader that exemplified both Huk socialist rhetoric and wartime-bred *pinay* empowerment. Culala was the only woman founder and elected member to the Military Committee of the Hukbalahap.[9] Culala's military rank afforded her the

[8] FilipiKnow, "The 10 Most Incredible Filipina Warriors of World War II," *FilipiKnow.Net*, Last Modified December 5th, 2018, Last Accessed December 21st, 2018, https://filipiknow.net/filipina-heroes-of-wwii/.
[9] Vina A. Lanzona, "Capturing the Huk Amazons: Representing Woman Warriors in the Philippines, 1940s-1950s," *South East Asia Research*, Vol. 17 No. 2 (July 2009), 134, 135.

title of Kumander Dayang-Dayang, a name attributed to a famous Moro princess that translates to "a Princess of the First Degree."[10] The title "Dayang-Dayang" thus had a deeper historical background that further reinforced her leadership position amongst the Huks. Culala began fighting against the Japanese immediately after their invasion of the Philippines, long before the Hukbalahap began to organize themselves as a military branch. When the Huk rebellion began, she and the auxiliary troops she organized added a significant branch to the Huk movement, leading to Calula becoming one of the four co-founders of the Huk organization in 1942, after the execution of its first leader, Crisanto Evangelista.[11] She served as the only woman elected to the Hukbalahap Mili1tary Committee, where she operated as the head of Huk guerrilla units situated in the East Pampanga District of Luzon.[12]

Culala is known for making do with what little resources and manpower she had—especially in the lesser-known Battle of Mandili. There, Culala staged an ambush to rescue her captured guerrilla soldiers from within the Japanese holding of the barrio of Mandili

---

[10] Unknown Author, "Dayang-Dayang: A Princess of the First Degree," *Dayang Dayang: Sulu Princess*, Last Modified 17th, 2009, Last Accessed December 21st, 2018, http://suluprincess.blogspot.com/.

[11] Alfred W. McCoy, ed., *An Anarchy of Families: State and Family in the Philippines* (Madison: The University of Wisconsin Press, 2009), 62-65.

[12] Tonette Orejas, "Last Living Woman Huk Leader Gets Pension," *Inquirer.Net*, Last Modified June 24th, 2014, Last Accessed August 4th, 2017, http://newsinfo.inquirer.net/613833/last-living-woman-huk-leader-gets-pension-back.

(Culala's hometown), and, with less than 140 men, was able to eliminate 40 Japanese officers and 68 police officers, pilfering the remaining Japanese resources from the battle for the Huk guerrillas.[13] Though Culala proved to be a great military leader and strategist, she experienced a great deal of scrutiny from her male Huk peers.

Accounts of those who worked with Felipa paint her in two radically different depictions: one as a strong leader who had a commanding presence, and another as an overbearing, haughty, conceited, and power-hungry woman who did not heed the Huk rules of conduct.[14] It would be the latter depiction that came to define (and plague) Culala's legacy. Eventually, Culula's behavior became so disruptive to the Huk movement that her comrades put her on trial, convicting her of both tyranny and stealing supplies from helpless barrios, resulting in her execution by firing squad for such unwanted "behavior."[15] The extravagant nature of her execution served to characterize Filipina *guerrilleras* as unstable women easily consumed by their own passions, and thus, detrimental to the resistance.

The draconian execution, and the paucity of reliable primary sources depicting Culala's actual personal-

---

[13] Leonard Davis, *Revolutionary Struggle in the Philippines* (New York: Palgrave Macmillan Press, 1989), 37.

[14] Davis, *Revolutionary Struggle in the Philippines*, 37.

[15] Luis Taruc (1967), He Who Rides the Tiger, Praeger, New York, 129.

ity and actions have reinforced the notion that Culala impeded rather than helped Huk guerrilla operations.[16] However, after the war ended, Huk women argued that Culala was demonized because she was a threat to the power and influence of her male peers, especially the chief of the Huks, Luis Taruc. In their eyes, the party worked deliberately to find the means of proving Culala's inability to lead or have a significant role in the Huk resistance.[17] The discrepancies in Culala's narrative reveal how gender hierarchies and a patriarchal culture defined the Huk movement.

The difficulty in finding solid resources on Culala, along with the surviving depictions of her "infamous" and "excessive" behavior that attack her based on characteristics attributed directly to her gender, reveal the excessive barriers of discrimination that Filipina guerrillas faced. Even in organizations that afforded women slightly more freedom and recognition, like the Huks, women like Culala—who held multiple privileges (wealth, mestiza caste) and demonstrated soldierly resilience—continued to be marginalized based on rigid gender conventions. Culala's sex ultimately prevented her from living long enough to witness the

---

[16] Marc V., "14 Amazing Fillipina Heroines You Don't Know But You Should," *FilipiKnow.Net*, Last Modified October 7th, 2018, Last Accessed December 22nd, 2018, https://filipiknow.net/greatest-filipina-heroines/.

[17] Cynthia G. Franklin, Ruth Hsu, & Suzanne Kosanke, ed., *Navigating Island and Continents: Conversations and Contestations in and Around the Pacific, Selected Essays, Vol. 17* (Honolulu: Colleges of Languages, Linguistics and Literature, University of Hawai'i, 2000), 8.

fruits of her labor—the liberation of the Philippines. Nonetheless, Culala remains the highest-ranked woman in the Huk resistance. As such, she should be remembered not only for her contributions to the underground resistance but also as a symbol for feminist Filipina empowerment.

Kumander Guerrero, Simeona Punsalan-Tapang of San Simon

Commander Guerrero, a grassroots socialist *guerrillera* who advocated for peasants' and farmers' rights prior, during, and long after World War II. This photograph shows a captured Guerrero in the custody of the Philippine government in Bataan-Zambales, circa 1948, courtesy of Rizal Library, Ateneo de Manila University.[18]

---

[18] This photograph shows a captured Guerrero in the custody of the Philippine government in Bataan-Zambales, circa 1948, courtesy of Rizal Library, Ateneo de Manila University.

Another example of exceptional Huk female leadership is Simeona Punsalan-Tapang. Punsalan's accomplishments on the battlefield earned her the title of *Kumander* Guerrero. She joined the Huk after learning that Japanese soldiers were notorious for kidnapping and raping Filipina women. To protect her fellow *pinays*, Punsalan spoke with Hukbalahap representatives in her village and joined their ranks.[19] Punsalan served in Hukbalahap Squadron No. 104 from November 1942 to December 1943, before being promoted to major in 1944 under the 1st Regiment, Second Battalion Staff, Regional Command No. 7.[20] As a political advisor and networking courier, Punsalan kept local villages informed of Japanese encroachment. She single-handedly secured the safety of local Filipinos and boosted their morale by regularly notifying them of victorious Huk raids that crippled Japanese storehouses and further entrenched the resistance.

As a courier, informant, spy, commander, soldier, and Huk recruiter, Punsalan served as an example of how, given the right opportunities, *pinays* had the potential to play a crucial role in liberating the Philippines. Indeed, as a result of her actions, Punsalan's legend spread quickly throughout the Huk movement.

---

[19] Lanzona, *Amazons of the Huk Rebellion*, 156.
[20] GMA News, "Last Living Huk Commander Passes Away a Day Before Her 93rd Birthday," *GMA News Online*, Last Modified July 2, 2015, Last Accessed December 18th, 2018, https://www.gmanetwork.com/news/lifestyle/content/514518/last-living-huk-commander-passes-away-a-day-before-93rd-birthday/story/.

She was especially known for her steely resolve on the battlefield, where she participated on the frontlines alongside her comrades. Supreme Chief of the Huks Luis Taruc once described Punsalan as "a big bodied woman with a man's strength, fond of wearing men's clothes and adept at handling an automatic rifle."[21]

And yet, even so, Punsalan still faced gender discrimination, often in the form of male guerrillas refusing to listen to her orders. On such occasions, Punsalan drew on both her experience as a leader of a patriotic resistance movement and her intimidating six-foot figure to put uncooperative subordinates in their place.

> My command on the front line was for us to {create} a V-formation but my second in command refused to follow my order. I pulled out my 37 cal. gun and pointed it to him. I said, 'Now you will have to follow my command. He did."[22]
>
> — Commander Punsalan

Despite the sexism *guerrilleras* faced, Punsalan's accomplishments and recruiting efforts did not go unno-

---

[21] ABS CBN Staff Writer, "Last Hukbalahap Commander Dies, Age 92," *ABS CBN News*, Last Modified July 3rd 2015, Last Accessed December 22nd, 2018, https://news.abs-cbn.com/nation/regions/07/02/15/last-hukbalahap-commander-dies-age-92.

[22] Interview. Tonette Orejas, "Woman Huk Commander's Wish: Care for Huk Vets," *Philippine Daily Inquirer*, Last Modified July 1st, 2014, Last Accessed December 18th, 2018, https://www.pressreader.com/philippines/philippine-daily-inquirer/20140701/281612418494661.

The late Commander Guerrero, aka Simeona Punsalan,
pictured here celebrating her 92nd birthday and speaking
on behalf of the Huk Veterans advocating for their service
benefits, July 2014.[23]

---

[23] Ligaya Caballes, "Simeona Punsalan Tapang, "Kumander Guerrero",
the last living Huk Kumander and proud Kapampangan, dies at 92,"
PinoyCulture.Com: Your Source for Everything Pilipino, Last Modified July
12th, 2015, Last Accessed December 18th, 2018,
http://pinoy-culture.com/simeona-punsalan-tapang-kumander-
guerrero-the-last-living-huk-kumander-and-proud-kapampangan-
dies-at-92/.

ticed, convincing other women—like Gloria Rivera—
to join the guerillas. Rivera, like Punsalan, feared that
the Japanese would try to rape her and, in an effort to
learn how to protect herself and her fellow *pinays*,
joined the Huk rebellion. Rivera would also rise
through the ranks and take command of her own
squadron.[24]

Kumander Guerrero's heroism and commitment to
the guerrillas would continue long after the war. Not
all Filipino soldiers and guerrillas would be granted
the appropriate recognition, veteran status, and benefits promised to its heroes, particularly those outlined
in the Nationality Act of 1940. The Rescission Acts of
1946 signed by President Truman made sure to deny
veterans' benefits to the Filipino troops who served
with the argument that the United States had paid
$200 million in cash to the Philippines after the war
for their sacrifices, money which the Philippine government never received.[25] The influence of American
foreign policy making would not end after the war.
The postwar Philippines economy functioned at the
beck and call of the United States, who continued to
manage the Philippines both by providing economic
support and by manipulating government seats in the

---

[24] Vina A. Lanzona, *Amazons of the Huk Rebellion: Gender, Sex, and Revolution in the Philippines* (Madison: University of Wisconsin Press, 2009),
158, 159.

[25] Congressional Record, *United States of America: Congressional Record: Proceedings and Debates of the 111th Congress, First Session* (Washington: United States Government Printing Office, 2009), 16040.

new Philippine government. This caused tension between the new democratic republic of the Philippines and other political groups, like the Huk and other socialist leaning parties.

After the war ended, Huk veterans began a legal battle against the Philippine government for compensation and recognition of their service. Unfortunately, it soon became clear that these Huk veterans would be unsuccessful. Indeed, because of their communist ties, Huk veterans were barred from participating in the newly formed Philippine government. This eventually forced them into hiding, where they would take up arms yet again as a guerrilla force, this time with the aim of liberating the neo-colonial Philippine state from American control. The United States continued to manage the Philippines after the war, regularly intervening in its domestic politics for the sake of "democracy." As a result, Huk guerrillas went uncompensated. Even worse, because they were portrayed in such a negative light by the neo-colonial Philippine state, their efforts to liberate the Philippines during World War II became increasingly underappreciated.

Kumander Guerrero, despite the negative connotations attached to the communist rhetoric of the Hukbalahap, would fight for the recognition of and pensions for surviving members of the Huk forces who fought throughout World War II until her death in

2015 at the age of 93.[26] By 2014, Punsalan had helped over one hundred Huk veterans apply for pensions and correct their military documents and records, using her thumbprint and a vast reservoir of memories about the Huk guerrillas as evidence of the major contributions that she and other resistance fighters made in the fight against Japan's occupation of the Philippines.[27]

Comfort Woman: Maria Rosa Henson

The fear of rape that spurred women like Punsalan and Rivera to protect themselves and join the resistance was well-founded. Eyewitness accounts reveal how Japanese soldiers targeted Filipinas throughout the villages and barrios of the Philippines. Such accounts of women being molested, beaten, kidnapped, and sometimes even mutilated by Japanese soldiers reveals the sexual violence women and children were vulnerable to in times of total war. Under Japanese occupation, women throughout the Pacific were forced to become sex labor-

---

[26] Tonette Orejas, "Last Woman Huk Leader Dies, Leaves Legacy of Dedication," *The Philippine Inquirer, Central Luzon*, Last Modified July 3rd, 2015, Last Accessed December 16th, 2018, http://newsinfo.inquirer.net/702422/last-woman-huk-leader-dies-leaves-legacy-of-dedication.

[27] Tonette T. Orejas, "Last Woman Huk Leader Dies, Leaves Legacy of Dedication," *Inquirer Central Luzon*, Last Modified July 3rd, 2015, Last Accessed December 21st, 2018, https://www.pressreader.com/philippines/philippine-daily-inquirer/20150703/281861527163822.

ers for the Imperial Japanese Army. Near the end of the war, when surrender seemed imminent, the Imperial Japanese Army ordered all "comfort women" killed, and all documents and "comfort stations" that might speak to their existence destroyed.[28]

Scholars estimate that roughly 200,000 women across during the Pacific War were forced into the sex slavery system implemented by the Imperial Japanese Army.[29] Many of these women survived the war, but few lived to pass on their stories during the early 1990s when international news caught wind of attempts by Asian women's nonprofit organizations to broadcast survivors' testimonies.[30] To this day, leaders of Japan's government and foreign relations, including Prime Minister Shinzō Abe, refuse to fully acknowledge the brutalities and exploitation of Asian women by the Imperial Japanese Army.[31]

Traditionally, women are not seen as combatants; they are lumped into the category of casualties of war.

---

[28] Eileen Yujoo Kim, *Korean Comfort Women: Political and Personal History Intertwined* (Berkeley: University of California Press, 1997), 43-45.

[29] Yoshimi Yoshiaki, *Comfort Women: Sexual Slavery in the Japanese Military During World War II* (New York: Columbia University Press, 1995), 91.

[30] Miki Y. Ishida, *Toward Peace: War Responsibility, Postwar Compensation, and Peace Movements and Education in Japan* (New York: iUniverse, Inc., 2005), 71.

[31] Tomohiro Osaki, "Abe Rejects Seoul's New Call for Apology On 'Comfort Women' Issue," *Japan Times*, Last Modified January 12th, 2018, Last Accessed December 21st, 2018, https://www.japantimes.co.jp/news/2018/01/12/national/politics-diplomacy/abe-rejects-kangs-new-apology-call-comfort-women-issue/.

Such terminology portrays Filipinas as silent, helpless, and nameless victims forced into the tumultuous violence born from war. Thus, *pinays* that were abused and victimized by Japanese male soldiers are depicted as unable to protect themselves, and unable to possess the strength needed to further the goals of the Philippine resistance. But such women who were "casualties and victims of war," and experienced rape, torture, or were killed, were not powerless bodies. Pinays held their own, exercising a kind of strength and agency that demonstrated their resistance, political defiance, and participation in the war effort.

Indeed, many of the Huk guerrillas were incredibly strong women who survived beatings, rape, and torture at the hands of Japanese soldiers. Maria Rosa Henson was only fourteen when the Japanese invaded the Philippines in 1941. According to Henson's autobiography, *Comfort Woman*, while she was gathering firewood near Fort Bonifacio, a group of Japanese soldiers seized her, upon which each took turns raping her.[32] She was later found by a local farmer who brought her to her family to heal and recover from the physical and psychological trauma of her encounter with the three Japanese soldiers.[33]

---

[32] Maria Rosa Henson, *Comfort Woman: A Filipina's Story of Prostitution and Slavery Under the Japanese Military* (New York: Rowman & Littlefield, 2017), 29.

[33] Kathryn J. Atwood, *Women Heroes of World War II: The Pacific Theater, 15 Stories of Resistance, rescue, Sabotage, and Survival* (Chicago: Chicago Review Press Incorporated, 2017), 101-103.

Maria and her mother eventually moved to the village Pampanga to escape the Imperial Japanese Army.[34] Pampanga had a sizable Hukbalahap presence, and Maria was soon recruited to serve as a message courier, whose tasks included gathering supplies from the local villagers to aid the resistance.[35] After several successful missions and close encounters with the Japanese, Maria was eventually arrested at a Japanese checkpoint and sent to a "comfort station," where she became a sex slave, or comfort woman, for the Imperial Japanese Army stationed near Pampanga. Every day in captivity, Maria was raped by multiple Japanese soldiers, anywhere from ten to thirty men in one day, who savagely beat and cursed at her.[36]

While in the comfort station, Maria overheard Captain Tanaka and his officers making a plan to attack Pampanga, her mother's home barrio.[37] The next day she was able to whisper a warning to an old man outside the fence of her compound. In turn, he warned the villagers so they may escape. When the Japanese officers discovered what she had done, they tied Maria up and beat her senselessly[38] Local guerillas later raided the comfort compound and freed Maria along with other comfort women and POWs.

---

[34] Atwood, *Women Heroes of World War II*, 101.

[35] Atwood, *Women Heroes of World War II*, 102.

[36] Henson, *Comfort Woman*, 37-59.

[37] Henson, *Comfort Woman*, 55.

[38] Henson, *Comfort Woman*, 59.

After her rescue, Maria lived with her mother for the remainder of the war. Her mother, Julia, worked everyday to help her daughter recover. Julia spoon fed her daughter and helped her to walk again. Because of the extreme extent to which the abuse Maria's experiences in the comfort station had taken on her physical and mental psyche, simple movements and daily activities became daunting, if not impossible, tasks for her.[39] She rarely left the house in fear of being recognized by Japanese officers. Maria would eventually physically recover, marry, and have children with another guerilla by the name of Domingo. However, after the Japanese occupation ended, the Huk rebellion would continue on, with the aims of ending monopolies on land redistribution, social inequality, and the continuing postcolonial American presence in Philippine affairs. Domingo would continue fighting alongside the Huk rebels, eventually leaving Maria and their children for both the Huk cause and another woman.[40]

Nearly fifty years passed before Maria would speak about her experiences during the war. In 1992, a radio program about World War II comfort women aired and caught Maria's attention. She came forward to tell her story, with the hopes that other Asian comfort women would no longer hide from the cultural shame produced by the violations their bodies endured. Because many Asian cultures are centered on patriarchal

---

[39] Henson, *Comfort Woman*, 61.
[40] Atwood, *Women Heroes of World War II*, 106, 107.

values, many comfort women felt the need to hide their pasts, feeling immense shame, as former sex slaves. Testimonies from Korea, Taiwan, China, and the Philippines describe these women as having intense and lingering socio-cultural notions that the violations of their bodies translated to shame and dishonor that was detrimental to theirs and their family's reputations.[41] Maria's bravery, which gave her the ability to speak about her experiences and narrate her role in the war, reveals the many-gendered-levels of wartime that are often glazed over. In doing so, Maria was not only able to serve her country and people by relaying the bravery and grit of wartime Filipinas, but she also opened up the sensitive conversation as to how Asian women should break out of the traditional female mold of pure and reserved wives and obedient daughters.

In 1993, Maria and a group of other comfort women, under the guidance and protection of the Task Force of Filipino Comfort Women and Asian Women Human Rights Council, sued the Japanese government for their crimes and were offered a small settlement from the Asian Women's Fund in 1995.[42] Many comfort women refused the Japanese government's mini-

---

[41] Yoshimi Yoshiaki, *Comfort Women: Sexual Slavery in the Japanese Military During World War II* (New York: Columbia University Press, 1995), 195, 196.

[42] Yuki Tanaka "Introduction," *Comfort Woman: A Filipina's Story of Prostitution and Slavery Under the Japanese Military* (New York: Rowman & Littlefield, 2017), xx, xxiii.

mal attempts at paying for their veterans' crimes. To this day, the Japanese government's blatant refusals to fully acknowledge their soldiers' past sexual crimes continues to be a topic of international debate for those concerned with human rights and war reparations.[43]

Maria Rosa Henson's roles as a female guerrilla, comfort woman, mother, daughter, and women's activist showcases the multitude of responsibilities that women, or "casualties of war," donned. Henson's narrative as a rape victim, turned survivor, turned activist, challenges the historical interpretation that women in war are powerless bodies. The women of this chapter, especially Henson and Culala, share and carry a gender-related cloud of shame. Culala is portrayed as a villainess, her accomplishments and role in the Huk resistance minimized to a supporting role, with the myth surrounding her execution serving as a warning to *pinays* who supposedly submit to their vanity. Henson's experiences as a comfort woman are associated with the stigma of losing one's feminine purity, and thus represents three of the casualties of female victimhood in war; social, psychological, and physical contamination. Both women and their experiences in traditional Filipino settings represent outliers during and after the war. Culala challenged the male hierarchy of leadership in the resistance, whereas Henson

---

[43] Atwood, *Women Heroes of World War II*, 108.

challenged intersecting gender and cultural stigmas associated with the purity of women's bodies. Both aggressively crossed boundaries limited to their sex and reconstructed notions of women's participation in war, thus making women visible actors rather than tallied casualties of war.

Protecting and safeguarding women's bodies was both a form of self-defense and patriotism. For *pinay guerrilleras*, the patriotism that fueled their dedication to the underground Huk resistance was inherently tied to the protection and safety of their womanhood. As patriotic liberators, Filipinas gained control over their bodies. Only when Filipinas possessed the means to defend themselves and oversee the conversations pertaining to their bodies, like Maria demonstrated, were Filipina soldiers of World War II considered controversial, unconventional, and simultaneously silenced, as evidenced by the blemished legacy of Culala's contribution to the Huk and the refusal of the Japanese government to publicly acknowledge the existence of comfort women.

Other *pinays* who served, unlike Calula and Maria, were aware of the potential consequences and backlash they would receive stepping into the battlefield and wartime politics. The *guerrilleras* who wished to participate in the liberation of their country navigated their roles with more precaution, and thus were the women who became the more glamorous mainstays of what little history of Filipina war heroes survives.

Photographed above is a bronze statue dedicated to the Filipina comfort women. The statue was initially erected in 2017 and placed on Roxas Boulevard overlooking Manila Bay. But soon after, the statue was taken down later in the Spring of 2018 under President Duterte's orders as he did not want to "offend" Japanese relations.[44]

---

[44] Gaea Katreena Cabico, "Gabriela Solons Seek Probe Into Removal of Comfort Woman Statue," *PhilStar News*, Last Modified May 10th, 2018, Last Accessed December 28th, 2018, https://www.philstar.com/headlines/2018/05/10/1813942/gabriela-solons-seek-probe-removal-comfort-woman-statue.

Chapter 3

The Glamorous *Guerrilleras*: Amazons of the Pacific Theater

A training still of a local Filipina Women's Auxiliary Corps in Manila. The official first Women's Auxiliary Service (WAS) was founded by Josefa Capistrano in Mindanao. The women pictured here were one of the first groups of Filipinas to train and serve as combat guerrillas, November 8th, 1941.[1]

---

[1] Doc Snafu, "(USAFFE) (Far East) Guerrilla Movement, Philippines, 1942-1945," *EUCMH Exposition Blog*, Last Modified July 17th, 2015, Last Accessed August 15th, 2018, https://www.eucmh.com/2015/07/17/usaffe-far-east-guerrilla-movement-philippines-1942-1945/.

The uniqueness of the Filipina World War II experience is revealed by the bold and untold accounts of female-led insurgencies during the Japanese Occupation. Surviving oral accounts and rarely written histories of Filipina guerrilla soldiers describe them as knowledgeable in combat and strategy—equal to their male peers. Filipina guerrillas organized and commanded insurgent units over expansive terrain. They also conducted much of the spy and infiltration work needed to provide stable communication and supply networks for the Philippine Underground Resistance and the remnants of MacArthur's American Allied intelligence throughout the Philippine archipelago. Filipinas served as couriers for guerillas, donated weapons and supplies, secretly housed and nursed Filipino and American POWs, and took up arms themselves. Filipinas of the resistance fought the Japanese on various fronts as *guerrilleras*, just as bravely as men did. Without their contributions, the liberation movement could quite possibly have failed.

Despite their valiance, the actions of women of color in the Pacific Theater are not as well-recorded as their male counterparts, frequently being subsumed by male-centric narratives of heroism, escape, and intrigue. Women who bravely fought within male-dominated insurgencies and the arena of war politics faced unique challenges and difficulties made more pressing by their gender, including the threats of capture, rape,

Mrs. Fuentes Arrives From The Philippines

PORTLAND, OREGON — Mrs. Claire Fuentes, wife of Mr. Manuel Fuentes, Assistant Superintendent of the Army Transport Service at Fort Mason, was the recipent of the Asiatic-Pacific Campaign Ribbon awarded by General MacArthur to civilians in the Philippines who by their courage

MRS. CLAIRE FUENTES

and intrepidity in helping the internees during the Japanese oppression in the Islands, facilitated the liberation of the Philippines. Mrs. Fuentes was jailed in Fort Santiago and tried by Japanese court martial, sentenced to prison and given by the Japanese Military all the maltreatment imaginable because of her connection with the underground resistance and because she helped the American internees in Santo Tomas. She arrived in this country early in May with her infant daughter Daine, and is at present vacationing with her parents in Portland, to join her husband later in San Francisco, California.

Claire Fuentes was a guerrilla who aided the POWS at the Santo Tomas Internment Camp. She was captured by the Japanese and jailed at Fort Santiago. She survived the war and the abuse from the IJA. In the article above published in *The Philippines Mail*, Claire went on to receive the Asiatic-Pacific-Campaign Ribbon Award from General MacArthur for her contribution as a *guerrillera*, circa May 1945.[2]

torture, enemy fire, and death. Additionally, women experienced constant verbal consternation from their male peers born from gender-based anxieties.

As American studies scholar Denise Cruz describes in her book *Transpacific Femininities: The Making of the Modern Filipina*, wartime Filipinas who worked tirelessly in the ranks of the resistance movement, although deemed patriotic,

---

[2] Staff Writer, "Mrs. Fuentes Arrives From the Philippines," *The Philippines Mail*, May 1945, Microfilm, John Steinbeck Public Library, Salinas, California.

were both underrepresented amongst their male peers and often designated to roles that matched familial conventions seen in traditional Filipino patriarchal households: mothers, sisters, or caregivers. If Filipinas wished to liberate their country from the Japanese occupation, they also had to risk the social criticisms of their male peers, who held steadfast to the *machismo* values exercised at nearly every rank and file of the underground resistance. Filipina guerrillas who took on leadership positions during the war, therefore, had to demonstrate and perform the preferred characteristics of the ideal Filipina to participate in the war and be deemed a Philippine patriot by her peers.

Many of the accounts of Filipina guerrillas that do survive—and are most celebrated—often emphasize women who both represented ideal Filipina beauty standards of the period and took on the preferred characteristics of the attentive nurse, adoring mother, and lover. Although performing such an assemblage of roles is a daunting and incredible feat during wartime, it is also true that such roles upheld certain patriarchal values. But there is a part of this story that is less well--known. Indeed, many of these "ideal" Filipina women also contributed to the resistance in ways that challenged rather than appeased the patriarchy. The most revered of these *guerrilleras* were the military heroines, or "Filipina Amazons," who took to task and reformed traditional standards of Philippine beauty, familial structure, and social patriarchy, whilst also conducting soldierly subterfuge and formulating battle strategies. These Filipina Amazons are often the most celebrated Filipinas in narratives written about the Philippines' fight against Japanese occupation, in part because they represent a perfect blend of wartime romanticism and culturally dominant notions of Filipino conventions of female beauty and grace. In their own ways, these glamorous guerrillas reshaped notions of intra-ethnic gender relations and demonstrated outright women's capacities and major potential as community influencers and military leaders.

Colonel Yay Panlilio

A photograph of Panlilio at the guerrilla Marking headquarters at the close of the war, circa 1945.[3]

> "I wrote into my column advice for the women: 'Let your children look back and remember how their mothers faced the war'."[4]
>
> — Colonel Yay Panlilio

---

[3] 17.21 Women, "Yay Panlilio," *Deskgram*, Last Modified July 2018, Last Accessed December 23rd, 2018,

https://deskgram.net/explore/tags/yaypanlilio.

[4] Yay Panlilio, *The Crucible: An Autobiography by Colonel Yay, Filipina American Guerrilla* (New Brunswick: Rutgers University Press, 1950).

As a trained journalist concerned with Filipino national politics and women's rights, Yay Panlilio's contributions to the early strands and waves of resistance drew heavily from her own grassroots ideologies. With a background in muckraking journalism, and as a politically savvy radio host turned *guerrillera*, Panlilio added layers of glamour, sensationalism, and long overdue sentiments of Filipino nationalist language to promote the goals of the guerrilla resistance. Her autobiography, *The Crucible: An Autobiography by Colonel Yay, Filipina American Guerrilla*, relays her daring military exploits during the war in a manner akin to an action-packed film. In combination with her *mestiza* looks and tumultuous love affair with the leader of the Marking guerrillas, her autobiography paints a romanticized telling of the guerrilla movement that caters to the overemphasis, as scholar Denise Cruz argues, of the generalized roles and experiences of women during wartime.[5]

Yay Panlilio is one of the most celebrated female leaders of the resistance. Her personal autobiography remains the key written resource in terms of depicting the rare experiences of Filipina insurgents who held high military ranks. Panlilio, a biracial Filipino American *mestiza*, was revered by both the Filipino and American soldiers she oversaw. Her motherly treatment and command of her troops, her beauty as a fair

[5] Denise Cruz, *Transpacific Femininities: The Making of the Modern Filipina* (Duke University Press, 2012), 175.

skinned, racially mixed *mestiza,* combined with her American and Filipino upbringing and her straddling of two cultural fronts in the Pacific Theater, made her the ideal woman of war. However, Panlilio's autobiography does not highlight her own achievements as a commander of male troops, or her other contributions to the war effort as an outspoken journalist, *guerrillera* spy, and Filipino patriot. Instead, her account of the war puts the efforts of men, like her love interest colonel Marcos V. Agustin, front and center. Nonetheless, she often describes herself, perhaps without being conscious of her tendencies of kowtowing to Agustin's violent and ego-centric whims, as a leader of the Marking Guerrillas.

Her words and submissive intonations, found throughout her narrative of the war, may have, as Denise Cruz argues, been the only way to attract audiences to listen to her story, by painting herself as a damsel running into the trenches of war, finding love, and in the end, running off victorious and married to the man she supported on the front lines.[6] Whatever Panlilio's intentions were in relegating herself to the traditional and overly romanticized role as lover and dutiful wife, her autobiography remains a valuable account of *pinay* history. Her written account is a primary source that highlights her role as a colonel and encounters with other Filipina guerrillas, showcasing the

---

[6] Cruz, *Transpacific Femininities,* 167-178.

existence of military engaged women and leaders while further demonstrating, in the manner in which she chose her words, the various gendered barriers strong women faced head-on in male-centric wartorn terrains.

> "Filipinos will die for love. Americans will die for principle. I am half-and-half. I die the same way."[7]
>
> — Yay Panlilio

Yay Panlilio was born and raised in Denver, Colorado, in 1913. She was a *mestiza*, a woman of mixed-race; her father was Irish-American, and her mother was Filipina. Panlilio, proud of her mixed heritage, described herself as a woman who encapsulated both cultures. Yay would eventually leave the United States as a teenager and embarked on pursuing a career as a serious radio news correspondent and journalist in the Philippines.[8]

Panlilio worked in Manila as a reporter for the *Philippines Herald* before the war. Later, when the threat of invasion was imminent, she became sworn in as a U.S. Intelligence agent. When the war broke out in 1941, she requested to leave Manila and head with the army to Bataan. Her letters were denied their request and she was told to "stick around" in order to conti-

---

[7] Denise Cruz ed., Yay Panlilio, *The Crucible: An Autobiography by Colonel Yay, Filipina American Guerrilla* (Rutgers University Press, 2009), 63.
[8] Panlilio, *The Crucible*, ix.

nue reporting any Japanese movement in occupied Manila.[9] After consistent refusals from U.S. Intelligence chief officers like Captain Ralph Keeler, Panlilio decided she would practice her own style of resistance and declared herself a guerrilla.

Panlilio's initial guerrilla tactics involved her use of familiar newsmedia positions to facilitate propaganda against the Japanese. She used her radio broadcasts via KZRH Manila Radio to send coded messages hinting at information about nearby Japanese activity to the newly forming resistance movement.[10] Her messages were so cryptic that even General MacArthur was known to become frustratingly concerned with Panlilio's loyalties, not knowing what to make of Panlilio's radio efforts, especially as the Japanese directly monitored her every move and broadcast.[11] While working with KZRH, the Japanese secured intel regarding who managed the radio broadcasting. One of her acquaintances at the station became a recruit for the Japanese Military Intelligence, a man by the name of Taki. Over time Panlilio gave him false information about the whereabouts of American and Filipino rebels and guerrilla sympathizers, hoping she could bide enough time to send the Imperial Japanese Army off the scent of the Allies and guerrilla resistance in the Philippines.

---

[9] Denise Cruz ed., Yay Panlilio, *The Crucible: An Autobiography by Colonel Yay, Filipina American Guerrilla* (Rutgers University Press, 2009), 7, 8.
[10] Panlilio, *The Crucible*, 12.
[11] Cruz, *Transpacific Femininities*, 169-179.

Playing a double agent was risky, but *pinay* guerrillas like Panlilio were willing to sacrifice life and limb to bring about the liberation of the Philippines, knowing very well that torture, rape, and the murder of innocent relatives were possible consequences of their actions.

Panlilio was for some time able to avoid detection, but eventually, Japanese suspicions led to attempts at arresting her. Panlilio, having no time to lose, left Manila while in disguise with the help of sympathetic locals and other resistance contacts. They would provide Panlilio with freshly laundered women's clothing, makeup, and different male guides to disguise herself with in order to survive from one checkpoint to the next.[12] Yay escaped to the mountains and would hide in the hut of a farmer by the name of Igi, but soon after became afflicted with malaria. But fate would ensure that Panlilio would soon be called into service once more. While Panlilio was recovering from malaria, guerrillas under Colonel Agustin stumbled upon her location whilst searching for a secure place to hide. Within Igi's hut, they found a journalist-turned--guerrilla-resistance-fighter-in-the-making resting inside. Despite her illness, Panlilio was ready and willing to contribute something to the resistance.

Fearing that a Japanese patrol would find them, Panlilio urged the men to hide in the surrounding area

---

[12] Panlilio, *The Crucible*, 12-15.

and recuperate in order to avoid capture. These men were Marking's guerillas, a unit of resistance fighters led by Marcos V. Agustin.[13] From that point forward, Yay became an essential asset and member of Marcos'—also known as Markings'—guerrilla resistance.[14]

The official flag of the Marking Guerrillas as depicted by surviving veterans and their families' accounts.[15]

---

[13] Panlilio, *The Crucible*, 15.

[14] Panlilio, *The Crucible*, 21.

[15] The Marking guerrillas were established in the Sierra Madre Mountains under Colonel Hugh Straughn, a Spanish American War veteran. Eventually, Marking's guerrillas became an independent organization when Straughn was captured and killed in August of 1943. The Marking Guerrillas were seen as ruthless to both the Japanese soldiers as well as to those who opposed their rank and were known to engage in open conflict with the Hunters ROTC Guerrillas. Watawat.net, "The Wha-Chi and Other Guerrilla Groups and Units," *Watawat: Flags and Symbols of the Pearl of the Orient Seas*, Last Modified 2017, Last Accessed December 17th, 2018, http://www.watawat.net/the-wha-chi--and-other-guerrilla-groups-and-units.html.

For two years she would live in the jungle and fight with the guerrillas. She survived her bout with malaria, among other jungle related ailments, and countless injuries from Japanese attacks. Unfortunately, Yay would fall into an abusive and demanding relationship with Colonel Marking while going through the emotional pains of being separated from her three children from a previous marriage, while they were kept hostage by the Japanese.[16] All of these experiences were compounded by the gendered guerrilla hierarchies she as a woman faced within a secluded and male-dominated total war environment.

Yay dealt with the sharp and stubborn tongues of male guerrillas who despised the idea of taking orders from a woman. One guerrilla by the name of Ming Javellana lobbed an underhanded comment at Yay after she gave orders for sleeping arrangements, complaining that "We fight. We don't eat. We don't sleep... And now we take orders from a woman."[17] Yay understood the gendered biases men had of women, especially in wartime, believing they were a detriment to the resistance, possibly even as detrimental as a double agent. Markings' men, Yay described, "hid their disgust behind blank faces: They could see dainty horns coming out from my temples, a forked tail curl about one ankle."[18] Being able to hold one's chin high while

---

[16] Panlilio, *The Crucible*, 10.

[17] Panlilio, *The Crucible*, 15, 19.

[18] Panlilio, *The Crucible*, 18-20.

under Japanese fire and taking bitter sexist insults from one's own "comrades" on a regular basis made the life of a *guerrillera* a personal and gendered war-zone; a war zone where women's social marginalization became magnified, multiplied, and compounded with the daily terror of total war.

The desperate mental state, as well as the harrowing physical toll experienced by constantly malnourished guerrilla fighters, that had to be at any moment ready for orders to raid a Japanese camp, or to pick up and evade a surprise Japanese attack, are viscerally described by Panlilio's journalistic flair and knack for writing in her memoir. Panlilio describes being in such close proximity to the Japanese army that she always had to be in the mindset to be prepared to shoot herself in order to avoid capture and interrogation because she feared she would divulge too much critical information under torture.[19] At one point, while escaping enemy fire, Panlilio describes how she and the remnants of a splintered group of Markings guerilla's only chance of survival meant climbing down a cliff face, without any of the necessary tools to do so safely. After this attack, Panlilio and her men survived starvation and being routed by the Japanese thanks to the kindness and support of local villagers they encountered.[20]

Panlilio's detailed autobiography provides an excellent depiction of life as a guerrilla during the Japanese

---

[19] Panlilio, *The Crucible*, 200.
[20] Panlilio, *The Crucible,* 74-78.

occupation, and in addition shows how involved women were in the resistance movement, even outside of the Hukbalahap party. Panlilio's mentions of several 'girl fighters' that she came across provide first account evidence of the Filipina *guerrilleras* who fought alongside their male peers. In particular, Panlilio praised the *guerrillera*, Captain Trinidad Diaz. Panlilio described Diaz's contribution to the underground resistance as essential to the momentum of the movement because similar to Celia Mariano Pomeroy and Commander Simeona Punsalan, she took on the task of recruiting informants while creating her own militant intelligence network that thwarted the local Japanese in her area of Binangonan.

Yay's brief account of Diaz praises not only her bravery but her cleverness in using her connections as courier and cashier at her community's local cement factory to effectively conduct her undercover missions.[21] Panlilio noted that Diaz's Home Guard unit patrolled her community's region and attacked Japanese soldiers. Diaz and her men hid the bodies of the soldiers in cement mixers to conceal any tracks leading to the efforts of her guerrilla branch. Diaz and her home guard of guerrillas also provided supplies such as food and ammunition to the Markings guerrillas through the network of contacts Diaz established.

---

[21] Panlilio, *The Crucible*, 31.

Eventually, the Japanese caught Diaz, tied her up, tortured her relentlessly (hanging her upside down, lashing her, and burning her), and executed her, but not before Diaz's *guerrillera* strategizing and networking galvanized further morale for the resistance.[22] Without Yay's humble mention of fellow *guerrillera*s like Captain Diaz, her sacrifices, like those of many other *pinays* who joined the resistance, might have been lost.

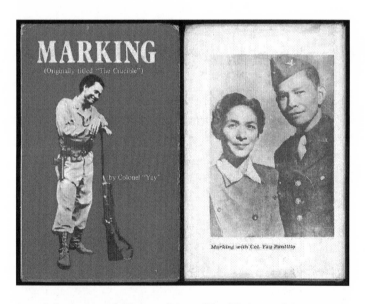

An original copy of a later edition of Panlilio's wartime memoir, *The Crucible*, with photographs of both her and her ex-husband Colonel Marking. The cover centers attention on Marking despite the wartime memoir based on Panlilio's experiences.[23]

---

[22] Panlilio, *The Crucible*, 30.

[23] PinoyKollector, "Marking," *Ebay Books*, Last Accessed December 25th, 2018, http://www.pinoycollector.com/ebay/books/March2008/.

WOMAN GUERRILLA CHIEF LAUDS ANGELENO OFFICER

It was a heroic crowd that sprang from vivid memories in the quiet hotel room.

There was the taciturn, brooding schoolmaster, who taught the Moros in peace and led and inspired them in war. There was the gallant American officer, who shared the privations and small fare of the guerrillas, and there were the guerrillas themselves, 200,000 of them, who came out of the barrios to unite their strength against the Japanese.

Had Price on Her Head

All of them were, and those still alive are, the friends of Mrs. Yay Panlilio, Filipina guerrilla leader, chief of staff of Marking's Fil-Americans, an army of almost a quarter of a million, who harried the Japs from the hills of the Philippines, the visitor said, to resist the enemy to the end.

Although she had a price on her head and was long separated from her three children, Edward, 8; Curtis, 3, and Rae, 12; although she suffered hardships and was frequently in serious danger, she preferred to talk about others rather than herself, in her room in the Baltimore, particularly about a Los Angeles Army officer, whose name cannot be disclosed because of censorship regulations, and Edward M. Kudner, the inland schoolteacher.

The Los Angeles officer was quoted by the visitor to have executed so splendidly his work as liaison officer with the guerrillas that he had been praised by four generals, headed by Gen. MacArthur, and including Gen. Carlos P. Romulo, Philippine Resident Commissioner.

He Kept the Faith

"Not every captain gets praised by four generals in a row," exclaimed Mrs. Panlilio.

"Some of his assignments were almost impossible to fulfill," she said, "yet, he managed, working 18 to 20 hours a day for a week, at a stretch, month after month.

holding the guerrillas steady and waiting for orders, answering headquarters' questions accurately, compiling data in less time than was demanded—never complaining, never losing, never doubting that the people back home in America were with him and all those like him when the rain poured cold and heavy, when he almost starved, but didn't quit."

Kudner, the visitor stated, in nearly 20 years of teaching won the love and confidence of the Moros, and, despite the unpredictable nature of the Moros, he was always safe among them.

She Was Born in Denver

Of herself, Mrs. Panlilio said that she was born in Denver and that she is half Filipina and half Irish. She went to the Islands when she was 18 and had been there 14 years when she was liberated, working during the years before the war on a newspaper in Manila.

Her three children, she said, had all seen Japanese cruelty.

Mrs. Panlilio plans to visit her mother in Auburn, Cal., before resuming her activities in behalf of Filipinos.

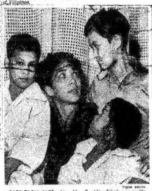

SAFE FROM JAPS—Mrs. Yay Panlilio, Filipino guerrilla leader, relaxes in Los Angeles with her children after fighting Japanese. From left to right, Edward, 9; Mrs. Panlilio; Curtis, 3, and Rae, 12. All escaped harm.

L.A. Times — August 1945

Article and L.A. Times clipping discussing Panlilio's war efforts, her *mestiza* background, and her motherly devotion to her family life.[24]

[24] This article is about Mrs. Yay Panlilio, who was a Filipino guerrilla leader, who helped the U.S. in their fight against Japan. The emphasis of depicting Yay as a mother and supportive guerrilla soldier rather than as her role as a colonel are the central themes of the short L.A. Times piece by the American author George Miller. L.A. Times August 1945. L.A. Times August 1945, "Mrs. Yay Panlilio," *Nehalem Valley Historical Society Online Archive*, accessed December 18, 2018, http://nehalemvalleyhistory.org/omeka/items/show/495.

Panlilio's experiences as a guerrillera serve as an example of the extent to which women were at the mercy of men's physical and verbal treatment, even among the slightly more egalitarian guerrilla units. Her relationship with the guerrilla commander, Marking, was both abusive and manipulative, yet, nevertheless, she remained loyal to him and supported him emotionally and militarily, eventually marrying him (they would later divorce). While many of the guerrillas under her command treated her with respect, some referring to her as 'mammy,' other officers became deeply resentful of her leadership position. Rather than acknowledging her skill sets as a multilingual and devoted journalist, intelligence officer, and soldier, some men in the Markings guerrillas, particularly out of contempt of being led by a female officer, accused her of securing her position as colonel as a result of her sexual relations with Colonel Marcos Agustin.

In popular Philippine narratives and film productions after the war, like *Cry Freedom* (1959), Yay is still remembered for her dramatized wartime romance with Agustin, labeled as a "girl guerrilla," and described as a secondary, supportive, figure overshadowed by Agustin's personality as a war hero. She would return to the United States alone to raise her three children and publish her wartime memoir in 1950. In 1951, Colonel Yay was awarded the U.S. Medal of Freedom with Silver Palm. And although her life and achievements are often constrained to the narrative that she was a doting mother, romanticized "girl guerrilla" persona, and an aide to the egocentric Colonel Marcos Agustin, Panlilio was, in actuality, a female literary and militant powerhouse in her own right.

Kumander Liwayway, a.k.a. Remedios Gomez

Another woman who embodied the ultra-feminine Filipina archetype while also exhibiting aggressive military prowess was Remedios Gomez. Known to wear lipstick and pristine get-ups while brandishing her weapons with polished nails and fashionable hair updos, Gomez was the epitome of Filipina beauty: a renowned beauty pageant barrio queen with brains and confidence to boot. She and her family became guerillas after her father was tortured and executed by the Japanese in 1942.[25] She was given the code name Liwayway, and, like other guerrilla women before her, was assigned to work as a medic. She would soon rise through the ranks, driven by her desire to exact revenge against the Japanese for her father's death, and was assigned the posts of commander over Squadron 3-V and chief of the Military Provision Division of Central Luzon.[26]

---

[25] Vina A. Lanzona, *Amazons of the Huk Rebellion: Gender, Sex, and Revolution in the Philippines* (Madison: University of Wisconsin Press, 2009), 152.
[26] Lanzona, *Amazons of the Huk Rebellion*, 153, 154.

In the Battle of Kamansi, she and her squad faced a larger Japanese force and succeeded in driving them back long after the other guerrilla squadrons had fled. As an officer, she also faced the endless task of providing for her men, which consisted of frequent travel to and from villages trying to rally sympathy and support for the resistance. Her men saw her as "a fearless and courageous leader unafraid to die."[27] Although Huk communist ideology defined passion, honor, dignity, and vengeance as strictly masculine emotions, Liwayway was seen by her male Huk comrades as capable of embodying both traditionally effeminate and traditionally masculine characteristics.[28] Indeed, her male comrades would often confront her and question her habits of putting lipstick on and wearing getups associated with social functions rather than battle. When one of her male peers, a man by the name of Katapatan, jested and insulted her with sexual innuendos, Liwayway challenged him to a duel, the result of which solidified her position as Huk woman leader.[29]

Her Huk *guerrillera* comrades, like Commander Simeona Punsalan-Tapang (aka Kumander Guerrero),

---

[27] Tonette Orejas, "Liwayway: Warrior Who Wore Lipstick in Gun Battles," *Inquirer.Net*, Last Modified May 17th, 2014, Last Accessed December 19th, 2018, https://newsinfo.inquirer.net/602758/liwayway-warrior-who-wore-lipstick-in-gun-battles.

[28] Lanzona, *Amazons of the Huk Rebllion*, 174.

[29] The specific details of the duel remain unknown. See Andrew G. Gomez, *Kumander Liwayway: Joan of Ark of the Philippines, Based on the True Story of Remedios Gomez-Paraiso* (Central Book Supply, 2009).

later on in life fondly remembered Liwayway's "feminine virtues."

> "Kumander Liwayway was truly beautiful and made us all wait while she put on make-up and polished her nails."[30]
>
> — Commander Simeona Punsalan

Liwayway's embodiment of the Philippine feminine archetype served as her way of displaying her pride as a Filipino woman who took charge of traditional gender tropes and transformed them into emblems of female leadership. She would continue to fight for the safety and inclusion of the Philippine peasants and farmers in the newly established Philippine Republic as a Huk underground resistance leader. She was caught twice by the Philippine Constabulary, and her husband and brother were killed by the new government. She was eventually released and cleared of her charges but always kept under close surveillance throughout the Cold War for her associations with the communist party. She died at the age of 95 in 2014, but her legacy as a Huk *guerrillera* who fought for her people's liberation on two fronts (World War II and

---

[30] Tonette Orejas, "Last Living Woman Huk Leader Gets Pension Back," *Inquirer.Net*, Last Modified June 24th, 2014, Last Accessed December 19th, 2018, https://newsinfo.inquirer.net/613833/last-living-woman-huk-leader-gets-pension-back. Interview with Commander Simeona Punsalan, "Kumander Guerrero of San Simon," Last Modified June 20th, 2014, Last Accessed December 19th, 2018 https://plus.google.com/+JenniferBichara/posts/MbCuptx3dK1.

post-war Philippine state formation) would be memorialized in her biography, written by her younger brother in 2009, and again in historian Vina Lanzona's book, *Amazons of the Huk Rebellion: Gender, Sex, and Revolution in the Philippines*.

Josefa Borromeo Capistrano

One of the surviving photographs of *guerrillera* Josefa Capistrano, founder of the Philippine Women's Auxiliary Corps.[31]

---

[31] "The 10 Most Incredible Filipina Warriors of World War II," *FilipiKnow.Net*, Last Modified December 5th, 2018, Last Accessed December 27th, 2018, https://filipiknow.net/filipina-heroes-of-wwii/.

Another Filipina trailblazer and powerhouse is Josefa Capistrano. Capistrano founded the Philippines' first Women's Auxiliary Service (WAS) in Mindanao. A Filipina-Chinese *mestiza* who was born to a family with prestigious political ties, Capistrano, like Yay, was a free-thinking Filipina ahead of her time. She strove to train and establish a purely female unit that would be recognized as an official unit of the Philippines Military.[32] The performance and skill of the WAS served as just one of the many landmark advances in women's rights and social presence in modern Philippines' History. Capistrano's WAS numbered three thousand militarily trained women skilled in combat, small industries (making bullets, textiles, bandages), nursing, and handling covert operations—particularly as spies—for both the American Allies and Filipino guerrilla networks.[33]

For Capistrano, all countrymen and women, from any class or background, were valuable assets to the resistance and the new Philippine Republic that Capistrano believed would come as a result of the liberation efforts of the guerrillas. On Mindanao, Capistrano exercised this belief, being assigned to lead and organize the "lay people," including women.[34] Capistrano's

---

[32] Keats, *They Fought Alone*, 221, 245.
[33] Evelyn Mallillin Jamboy, *The Resistance Movement in Lanao, 1942- -1945* (Coordination Center of Research and Development MSU-Iligan Institute of Technology, 2006), 74.
[34] Miguel Anselmo Bernad, *History Against the Landscape: Personal and Historical Essays About the Philippines* (Solidaridad Publishing House, 1968), 41.

belief in women's capabilities set her apart from those Filipinos who thought that women should be relegated to more traditional labor roles. It also aided the resistance's efforts against the Japanese, who had a gendered and limited purview of women's potential as subversives. Capistrano's belief in women's subversive capacity gave them an advantage in war, so long as they were given the opportunity—as Capistrano believed they should be—to contribute in ways that went beyond being a sideline "supporter."

> "Without the help of the people of the country, a guerrilla organization is doomed to fail."[35]
>
> — Josefa Capistrano

Capistrano was aware of the limited roles and opportunities Filipina women had in their households and communities, but, unlike her commanders and fellow male guerrillas, she foresaw the potential of women's inclusion in the liberation front, and more broadly to the Philippine Republic. Her female guerrillas successfully worked alongside Commander Wendell Fertig's guerrilla units in Mindanao throughout the war, proving to both American and Philippine military commands that women could match men in battle and in patriotic fervor.

---

[35] The Philippine Natural Historical Society, *The Journal of History: Volume 57, Philippine Natural Historical Society (2011)*, 253.

Despite the success and inclusion of Capistrano's female-led war industries and military units, the depiction of Capistrano's physical *mestiza* beauty received more notoriety than her capacity as a guerrilla leader. Wendell Fertig, famous American military engineer and commander of Filipino and American guerrillas in Mindanao, made sure to downplay Capistrano's military leadership in his autobiographical account made during the war, always referring to her as Nick Capistrano's "lovely wife."[36] At other points, she was described as "a mestiza of lustrous beauty whose skin had that creamy tone that only the slims of highborn Chinese have. Josefa always looked clean and delicate as a flower at dawn."[37]

Like other depictions of *pinay* guerrilleras, Fertig highlighted Capistrano's beauty as a mestiza, her family's affluence, and her ties to her esteemed husband rather than designating her vital role as a spearheading organizer and leader in her own right amongst the Mindanao guerrillas.[38]

Long after the war passed, Capistrano continued to argue for her female unit's recognition as an official branch of the Philippine Army. Thanks to Capistrano's headstrong perseverance in proving women's capabilities, particularly in instances of total war, Fili-

---

[36] Nick Capistrano was a wealthy lumber owner. See John Keats, *They Fought Alone: A True Story of an American Hero* (Echo Point Books and Media, 2015), 388.

[37] Keats, *They Fought Alone*, 130.

[38] Keats, *They Fought Alone*, 210, 420.

pinas were allowed a foot into the door of the postwar Philippines, allowed to expand both their career choices and their responsibilities as Philippine citizens. On par with men, Filipinas were seen as just as able to protect their country and bear the official badge of a warrior and patriotic soldier. Capistrano's legacy included her contribution to the war as a *guerrillera* and organizer of her female guerrilla units, culminating in the formation of the WAS as an official branch of the Philippine Military Armed Forces. It would be renamed the Women's Auxiliary Corps in 1963.[39]

Nieves Fernandez

While Capistrano and Panlilio were praised and remembered for traditional notions of Filipina mestiza beauty, other popular *guerrillera* narratives preserved were those of women who held other attributes associated with the ideal Filipina matriarch. The other aspect of Filipina womanhood valued by traditional gend er norms included the role of the motherly teacher. Nieves Fernandez is one such female guerrilla that embodied the strong Filipina patriot and military leader while donning the lifeway of a maternal precep-

---

[39] William B. Depasupil, "Women's Auxiliary Corps Unmanned After 50 Years," *The Manila Times*, Last Modified July 5th, 2013, Last Accessed August 2nd, 2017, http://www.manilatimes.net/womens-auxiliary-corps-unmanned-after-50-years/16088/.

tor. As one of the lesser known Filipina guerrilla leaders of the Pacific War, her story, like Kumander Liwayway's, has either been retold with romanticized wartime embellishments or been nearly glazed over into complete obscurity.

Few resources document Fernandez's guerrilla activity. Those that survive include sparse recollections of the soldiers who fought alongside her and the local communities of Tacloban on the island of Leyte that she sought to protect. Prior to the outbreak of the war, Fernandez lived as a simple school teacher.[40] Her first physical altercation with the Japanese that pushed her to take a more aggressive stance to defend her homeland involved a scuffle where the lives of her students were threatened. Imperial Japanese soldiers had gone through Fernandez's town and came around to the small school where she taught, threatening to take away her students. In the heat of the scuffle, she retaliated by shooting at the Japanese soldiers with her homemade shotgun.[41] Described as a skilled marksman and bolo fighter, Fernandez gained the respect of native locals, led her own unit of men into battle, and was so successful in taking out Japanese patrols that

---

[40] FMA Academy, "International Women's Day – Nieves Fernandez," *Filipino Martial Arts Academy: Certified and Comprehensive Instruction in the Filipino Martial Arts*, Last Modified March 8th, 2016, Last Accessed August 15th, 2018, http://fmaacademy.com/tag/captain-nieves/.

[41] Marc V., "14 Amazing Fillipina Heroines You Don't Know But You Should," *Filipiknow*, Last Modified July 27th, 2014, Last Accessed August 15th, 2018, http://www.filipiknow.net/greatest-filipina-heroines/.

the Japanese stationed in Tacloban placed a hefty 10,000-peso bounty on her.[42]

Fernandez, like other guerrillas throughout the Philippines, relied on makeshift weapons such as the "paltik" (a homemade shotgun made of gas pipes), bolos (a single-edged large knife), homemade grenades (casings filled with old nails) and whatever items she and the one hundred and ten guerrillas under her could pilfer from the Japanese.[43] Fernandez lived until her nineties, living the last years of her life in Tacloban. The sole surviving pieces of evidence depicting her heroics are a photograph and a small 1944 American newspaper article depicting her guerrilla contributions prior to the arrival of General MacArthur at Leyte.[44]

Wartime always produces a desperate and immoral landscape. Women in the Philippines faced additional threats compared to their male peers, which stemmed specifically from the traditional assumptions regarding the weakness associated with women. Women and children, throughout many world histories of war and conquest, experienced violent acts of subjugation like

---

[42] FMA Academy, "International Women's Day – Nieves Fernandez."

[43] Unknown Author, "School Ma'am Led Guerrillas On Leyte," *Lewiston Daily Sun*, October 26th, 1944, Last Accessed August 15th, 2018, http://www.michaeldsellers.com/blog/2017/02/11/looking-for-info-on-captain-nieves-fernandez-wwii-guerrilla-leader-in-leyte-philippines/.

[44] Michael Sellers, "Captain Nieves Fernandez – WWII Guerrilla Leader in Leyte, Philippines," Last Modified February 11th, 2017, Last Accessed August 15th, 2018, http://www.michaeldsellers.com/blog/2017/02/11/looking-for-info-on-captain-nieves-fernandez-wwii-guerrilla-leader-in-leyte-philippines/.

Fernandez is photographed here demonstrating to an American soldier how to effectively disable a Japanese soldier with the Philippine long knife, the bolo. Circa November 7th, 1944.[45]

rape, molestation, torture, physical and psychological abuse, and enslavement. Asian women throughout the Pacific Theater were forced, under terrifying circumstances, to obey the Japanese invaders or suffer the consequences of war. But despite the atrocities committed against Filipinas by the Japanese Imperial Army, Filipinas like Nieves Fernandez still chose to fight

---

[45] Rare Historical Photos, "Captain Nieves Fernandez Shows To an American Soldier How She Used Her Long Knife To Silently Kill Japanese Soldiers During Occupation, 1944," *Rare Historical Photos: Southeast Asia*, Last Modified June 21st, 2014, Last Accessed December 27th, 2018, https://rarehistoricalphotos.com/captain-nieves-fernandez-1944/.

bravely alongside their male counterparts. Their histories reveal that women were able, efficient, and self--driven leaders of the guerrilla resistance, regardless of the risks.

The "extraordinary" Filipina amazons of war discussed in this chapter are those *pinays* who matched a specific and preferred archetype—that of the ideal Filipina war hero. The most celebrated women of the guerrilla resistance aligned with the desired physical beauty standards, maternalistic personalities, and traditional gender roles and conventions afforded to Filipino women at midcentury. *Pinays* who straddled these immense expectations in gender performance within patriarchal war zones, like *guerrillera* leaders Panlilio and Liwayway, survive in the historical memory of war-torn Philippines as untouchable, ultra-feminine, modest, and pure; all the ideal standards expected of a humble acquiescent Filipina patriot.

But, at the same time, emphasizing such exceptional Filipina guerrilla heroes denies equal recognition to other *pinays* who were more "ordinary" in terms of their beauty, social class, and family lineage, and are not always depicted within the gendered backdrop of war as mothering supportive figures or caregiving sisters. Only recently have we recovered the accomplishments of the "ordinary" Pinay guerrillas discussed in the following chapter. These were Filipina heroines whose narratives lack the glamour associated with romantic Filipino and American notions of the *mesti-*

za traditional beauty. The dichotomy of their humble "ordinariness" and extraordinary wartime experiences demonstrates the silent and less visible ways in which *pinays* obtained female empowerment. Taken together, the politically radical and vocal *guerrillera* Huks discussed earlier, the glamorous *pinay* amazons highlighted in this chapter, and the everyday Filipinas detailed in the following chapter, represents a new standard—a new mold—for the model Filipina patriot.

Chapter 4

Filipina American Veterans: Recovering the Extraordinary Feats of the Ordinary Pinays

An advertisement channeling the maternalistic grace and peaceful aura associated with Filipino women's traditional roles as gentle matriarch overseeing the Filipino recruited troops training in California. The ad was sponsored by the Filipino American fraternal organization, the Caballeros De Dimas-Alang, found in a local Filipino American Newspaper in Los Angeles meant to build up support for the Fllipino troops abroad, circa 1942, Filipino American Collections, Courtesy of the Cultural Center of Guadalupe.[1]

[1] Filipino American Collections, Courtesy of the Cultural Center of Guadalupe, California.

Focusing on the untouchable heroes who match all of the famous literature's great expectations and depictions of war, liberty, and adventure often narrows our vision and hinders our ability to see all those champions who opted for a more "ordinary" life. This includes the women who came from less prominent lineages, who did not don the ultra-feminine Filipina mystique, were non-*mestizas*, and who left espionage missions to make a home and raise their family. These "ordinary" women, who could so easily be our neighbors, aunts, or grandmothers, are too often overlooked in our search for heroes.

The *pinay* guerrillas who survived the war and laid down their weapons found that they were forced to return to social conditions similar to what they had known before the war. Marriage, family, and possibly continuing one's education were the routes available to Filipinas still restricted to the patriarchal cultural norms that the Philippines at midcentury embraced. They immigrated, lived normal lives, married and had children, and didn't discuss their efforts until decades later. Even then they still argued that their roles were small and that the men who commanded them or delegated and oversaw their actions were the real heroes, unable to see themselves in a similar light. In truth, these women were assigned to protect families, sent coded messages, and worked as undercover agents scoping Japanese military stations. They participated in the resistance despite the risk it posed to themselves in the form of rape and torture, and despite the extent to which their actions endangered their families and friends. Indeed, because these women had families, they often had much more at stake. If they were caught, they risked shaming their family name. And yet, despite these hindrances, these women still met the war head-on.

Josefina Veluya-Guerrero

Photographed above is of *guerrillera* Josefina Guerrero posing for her carnet (international customs/international documents) photo, she was also known as 'The Leper Spy,' circa 1970.[2]

---

[2] Photograph of Josefina Guerrero, *from the Hoover Institution Archives,* Stanford, California.

The "ordinary" women who thrived within the resistance were often the antithesis of the classic Filipina amazon. Unlike the amazons, who were worshipped for their *mestiza* attributes, ordinary Filipina *guerrilleras* were often marginalized *because* others believed them to be substandard, either physically or otherwise. Ironically, such marginalization often made these women more effective operatives and spies. Indeed, those relegated to the bottom rung of the social caste system in traditional colonial Southeast Asian communities, such as the indigenous groups (for example the *Igorots* or *Negritos*), landless peasants, or even those afflicted with physical or medical handicaps, could more easily travel from one town to another province or barrio, often left untouched by both enemy surveillance and the locals' attention. One such individual, Josefina Veluya-Guerrero, who suffered from leprosy, used social ostracization to her advantage. Her isolated status allowed her to work beneath Japanese radar after they invaded and captured Manila in 1942.[3]

Throughout the Philippines in the early twentieth century, lepers were excluded from social and daily public spaces. Filipina/o lepers were forced to carry signs stating that they had the disease. Others were forced to carry a bell on their body and clothes so that people could hear them approaching, giving them the time to flee and avoid "catching" the illness them-

---

[3] Ben Montgomery. Leper Spy: *The Story of an Unlikely Hero of World War II* (Chicago Review Press, 2016), 20.

selves. For other unfortunate souls afflicted with the condition, they were placed into "leper colonies" away from the rest of society so as to isolate the disease.[4]

Fortunately, Josefina was able to avoid being sent to a leper colony, receiving private treatments that kept her illness secret from her community.[5] However, when the Japanese attacked Manila, she was unable to continue receiving treatment and her condition began to deteriorate. With both her country afflicted by Japan's occupation and her body in dire straits, Josefina believed that she did not have much time left to live. Her sense of desperation, combined with the isolation she felt like a leper and the dwindling hopes she had for her country's liberation, influenced her decision to join the resistance. She decided to—instead of allowing her condition to define her remaining time left looking and feeling like any other "ordinary" woman—use the stigma associated with her illness to her advantage to avoid Japanese suspicion and contact.

Josefina's primary roles for the resistance was as a courier. She carried intel from Manila to guerrilla camps stationed in the forests and mountain provinces, often hiding the notes twisted and wrapped within her hair as she styled it into a chignon or hair bun.[6] Without proper treatment, Josefina's illness became more visible, which she continued to use to her advan-

---

[4] Montgomery. *Leper Spy*, "Chapter: Volunteer."

[5] Montgomery. *Leper Spy*, 26.

[6] Montgomery. *Leper Spy*, "Chapter: Spies."

tage. Japanese guards refused to search her once they saw the "leper marks" on her arms and rushed her through checkpoints out of fear of contracting leprosy themselves. As more American soldiers began to make some headway in infiltrating Philippine shores, Josefina's courier operations extended beyond the guerrilla camps to working directly with USAFFE.

One of her more dangerous assignments included mapping enemy gun placements. Her maps allowed American bomber pilots to strategically coordinate aerial attacks, which significantly weakened Japanese cover and artillery stations. Josefina went to great lengths to obtain much-needed intel, so much so that she made a thirty-five-mile trek under heavy fire to give the Allies a map of the exact locations of Japanese mines and traps in the area.[7] Josefina's roles as courier and cartographer served as great assets to the liberation of the Philippines. Her sacrifices, bravery, and overall impact as a resistance intelligence office challenged if only temporarily, the social "taint" attached to leprosy.

After the war, the United States government awarded Guerrero with the Medal of Freedom with Silver Palm and welcomed her to the United States with a visitor's permit to live in a leprosarium in Louisiana,

---

[7] Colette Bancroft, "Ben Montgomery's 'Leper Spy' An Extraordinary True Story of WWII," Tampa Bay Times, Last Accessed December 25th, 2018, https://www.tampabay.com/features/books/ben-montgomerys-leper-spy-an-extraordinary-true-story-of-wwii/2294553.

where she received treatment for her condition and eventually was able to keep her disease dormant.[8] Although she faced multiple threats of deportation, Josefina was eventually awarded citizenship, and lived a simple life in San Francisco and then finally in Washington D.C., where she would settle permanently.

Joey, as she would be called by her American friends, would never speak about her espionage and heroic efforts as a *guerrillera*. To Joey's friends and neighbors in her later years, she was known only as a "humble and plain woman."[9] She lived the last leg of her elderly career as a well-to-do American citizen who worked for seventeen years as an usher for the Kennedy Center. She died in 1996 at the age of sixty-eight, leaving little to no remnants of her wartime memories as a "leper spy." It would take a trained and renowned journalist named Ben Montgomery to piece together her turbulent life in the Philippines and her quiet post-guerrilla career in the United States, revealing what we now know about this extraordinary "ordinary" woman.

---

[8] Cristina DC Pastor, "How the WWII Hero Josefina Guerrero Struggled with Deportation," *The FilAm: A Magazine for Filipino Americans in New York*, Last Modified November 26th, 2016, Last Accessed December 20th, 2018, https://thefilam.net/archives/22758.

[9] Montgomery. *Leper Spy*, "Chapter: Everything Is In Readiness."

Corporal Magdalena Leones

Photographed above is Magdalena Leones, one of the highest honored Filipina American World War II veterans, circa 1940s.[10]

Magdalena Leones is another Filipina guerrilla who dared the trek across the Pacific after the war in search of a simple life and humbler career. Born in the mountain province of Kalinga of Northern Luzon, Magdalena grew up in a Protestant household, in mountains turned upside down by the war. In 1942, when the Imperial Japanese Army invaded the Philippines, Magdalena was captured and jailed by the enemy and placed

---

[10] Xiao Chua,"'Lioness of PHL guerilla spies' Maggie Leones to be buried with full honors," *GMA News Online*, Last Modified June 11th, 2016, Last Accessed December 27th, 2018, https://www.gmanetwork.com/news/lifestyle/content/573214/lioness-of-phl-guerilla-spies-maggie-leones-to-be-buried-with-full-honors/story/.

in a prison camp.[11] She was eventually released, only to see first hand the slaughter of her people and the violent occupation of her country. Seeing the unimaginable deaths and anguish the Japanese exacted upon her countrymen, Magdalena became a guerrilla. She headed to Manila and worked with a pocket resistance led by missionaries and leaders of the Emmanuel Co-operative Hospital in Manila to provide funding for the growing guerrilla resistance in the mountains to the north.

Magdalena and her team of resistance volunteers would soon be found out by the Imperial Japanese Army stationed in Manila. Magdalena received contact from a Lieutenant Colonel sent directly from the Australian Allied base, who, unbeknownst to her and her colleagues, was a double agent working for the Japanese. He tasked Magdalena with finding and securing the whereabouts and names of the resistance to the North in order to "help establish contact" between the Allies and the fledgling Philippine resistance.[12] While trying to accomplish this mission, the real representatives of the USAFIP-NL (United States Army Forces in the Philippines of Northern Luzon) captured Magda-

---

[11] Filipino Veterans Recognition Project, "On July 4th: Remember Acts of Courage, Uncommon Valor," Last Modified July 15tyh, 2018, Last Accessed December 26th, 2018, https://usa.inquirer.net/13616/july-4th-remember-acts-courage-uncommon-valor?utm_expid=.XqNwTug2W6nwDVUSgFJXed.1.

[12] Chua,"'Lioness of PHL Guerilla Spies' Maggie Leones To Be Buried With Full Honors," *GMA News Online*.

lena, believing *she* was the double agent. Upon hearing the truth of her circumstances, and the capture, torture, and execution of her pocket resistance community in Manila at the hands of the Japanese, Magdalena became incensed to join the USAFIP-NL and continued her "special mission." Her main task, once inducted into the USAFIP-NL by the famous Colonel Russell W. Volckmann, was to secure communications and networks between the mountain guerrilla resistance of Northern Luzon and the American command center housing MacArthur in Australia. This mission, according to her Silver Star commendation, included carrying radio reports, intelligence, and smuggling medicine and supplies to the guerrilla resistance in the mountains of Northern Luzon from Manila, right under the Imperial Japanese Army's noses and through Japanese claimed territories.[13]

Magdalena's espionage missions would eventually earn her the title of 'the Lioness of the Filipina Agents.'[14] Her various guerrilla exploits included everything from recording the names and numbers of Ja-

---

[13] Emil Guillermo, "Magdalena Leones Filipina WWII Silver Star Recipient, Who Aided MacArthur, Dies in California," *NBCNews.Com: Asian America*, Last Modified July 5th, 2016, Last Accessed December 25th, 2018, https://www.nbcnews.com/news/asian-america/magdalena-leones-filipina-wwii-silver-star-recepient-who-aided-macarthur-n603566.

[14] Tammerlin Drummond, "Filipina Silver Star Winner, Richmond Resident Magdalena Leones Dies at 95," Last Modified June 17th, 2016, Last Accessed December 26th, 2018,
https://www.mercurynews.com/2016/06/17/filipina-silver-star-winner-richmond-resident-magdalena-leones-dies-at-95/.

panese ships coming into port of La Union, smuggling money, learning Japanese in order to misdirect Japanese soldiers to prevent them from attacking Filipino civilians and guerrillas, spending two years finding radio parts to establish a connection to the Allies in Australia, and destroying Japanese airplanes with strategically placed bombs. She accomplished all this, and more while traveling the rugged terrain between occupied Manila and the mountain province guerrilla hideouts.[15] Her dedication and unrelenting grit fostered better coordination between the resistance and the Allies in Australia—allowing for a more unified liberation front and a streamlined supply chain—and provided intelligence on the various Japanese strongholds in Luzon. Her efforts weakened the Japanese to the extent that General MacArthur was finally able to return to the Philippines.[16]

Though the war was over and Magdalena had come out of it a hero, it had thoroughly transformed her. After the war—at the age of twenty-five—Magdalena became the only Asian woman to be given the US Silver Star for her espionage field work and gallantry in action during World War II. Only four other women

---

[15] Bea Pantoja, "Finding Magdalena," *Bea-Pantoja*, Last Accessed December 26th, 2018, http://www.bea-pantoja.com/finding-magdalena-leones/.

[16] Emil Guillermo, "Magdalena Leones Filipina WWII Silver Star Recipient, Who Aided MacArthur, Dies in California," *NBCNews.Com: Asian America*, Last Modified July 5th, 2016, Last Accessed December 25th, 2018, https://www.nbcnews.com/news/asian-america/magdalena-leones-filipina-wwii-silver-star-recepient-who-aided-macarthur-n603566.

in America's military history have been given such a badge of honor and prestige.[17] But unlike other *pinay* amazons of the resistance, who continued to bear arms and found positions in the new Philippine government or military, Magdalena chose a more traditional route for her future: to marry, have children, and put her espionage days behind her. Like Josefina Guerrero, Magdalena opted to immigrate to the United States with her family in 1969, settle in California and take on a career as a clerk for Pacific Bell. Like Guerrero, Magdalena rarely spoke of her past life as a resistance fighter and intelligence officer for the USAFIP-NL. Her own children and grandchildren were kept in the dark much of their lives regarding their mother's exciting, yet brief, time as a crucial underground agent of the resistance.

On June 16th, 2016, Magdalena Leones passed away at the age of 95. Magdalena, who transformed from a nun-in-training into a resistance fighter, and then later into a humble wife, mother, grandmother, and first-generation Filipina American, would finally be officially recognized for her courage and sacrifices as a true American citizen and veteran of World War II in 2009.[18] Under Obama's 2009 Equity Pay Act, World War II Filipino guerrillas and scouts who applied were given a lump sum of $15,000, which Mag-

---

[17] Leonardo Q. Nuval, *Remember Them Kindly: Some Filipinos During World War II* (Claretian Publications, 1996), 31-33.

[18] Guillermo, "Magdalena Leones Filipina WWII Silver Star Recipient."

dalena was more than qualified for. As part of the memorial services due to World War II heroines, Magdalena's body was flown to the Philippines in order to receive a full hero's welcome, burial, and send off in full military honors at the Hero's Cemetery in Fort Bonifacio, to be with the other brave men and women who served their country.[19]

Serapia Estojero Aremas

Samar *guerrillera* Sherry (Serapia) Aremas at the age of 26 on her college graduation day, wearing her own design and take on the traditional *mestiza* dress. In the following weeks from her graduation from Manila's Fashion School, Sherry would embark on a cargo ship towards her new life in Salinas with her husband Ricardo Aremas, both World War II veterans, circa 1946. Courtesy of the Aremas Family Personal Collection.

Serapia Aremas was a college student when Pearl Harbor was set aflame by the Japanese. Tension and anxiety in the

---

[19] Filipino Veterans Recognition Project, "On July 4th: Remember Acts of Courage, Uncommon Valor."

Pacific had been growing for quite some years, but with American military bases stationed throughout the archipelago, and the buildup and training of Filipino recruits over the last several years, Philippine citizens were optimistic about the safety and security of their country. But sirens and blaring announcements at Serapia's university requesting students to leave campus and return home in the early months of 1942 signified the end of normalcy and the start of the war. Rather than go home to her barrio near Tacloban, Serapia was recruited by the local guerrilla resistance, after which she acted as a maid for a prominent local family that was loyal to the Allied front and funded operations against Japanese forces under the command of Lieutenant General Shiro Makino, who had recently laid siege to Serapia's home island of Leyte.

Serapia's official papers as a guerrilla woman, undercover, for the Philippine Guerrilla Forces at Samar, under the commander and chief of the Northern Leyte Branch, Jose C. Santos, circa 1943. Courtesy of Aremas Family Personal Collection.

But the Imperial Japanese Army's (IJA) intelligence bureau soon found out about Serapia's host family and their connections.

> "The villagers said that their heads had been cut off. Their bodies were floating in the river. I left {my post} and went home to my family."

When asked how long she went into hiding from the IJA near Tacloban, Serapia responded that she was "[n]ot really hiding from them. We were living in a little [remote] barrio. My father made a little house and managed a little farm, along the river, close to town. A road was close enough to our homes that we [the villagers] could signal to each other using the sounds [*Serapia proceeds to knock on the table*] of the bamboo [posts] when they would see some Japanese. When you hear that sound [*she knocks again*] you and the people who lived on that road, had to go away from that road. The people who did the signal were officers [guerrillas]. A husband and wife [who were guerrillas] on that road were killed. They [the Japanese] made a hole and put the husband and wife in there, buried alive."

She continued to support the war effort by volunteering for the USAFFE once MacArthur's forces secured their position after the Battle of Leyte. As a volunteer clerk, Serapia oversaw, packaged, and delivered supplies to local Filipino families on Leyte. It was here where she would meet her husband, a Filipino supply sergeant from the United States named Ricardo Aremas who was also assigned to the Allied supply warehouse. Serapia's daily duties included checking up on visiting families-in-need and reading through their applications for medical supplies and food rations.

Photographed above are a sample of the types of food rations that Philippine volunteers like Serapia would organize and hand to war ravaged families in Leyte.[20]

---

[20] Tessie Jayme, "Red Cross In Manila," *Black Clouds In Manila*, Last Modified March 2014, Last Accessed December 28th, 2018, http://blackcloudsinmanila.com/Red-Cross.php.

USAFFE aides like Serapia organized, delivered, and managed the paperwork regarding the food and medical supplies. Filipina nurses and volunteers for the Red Cross as pictured above shows the contributions of Filipina nurses and assistants packaging supplies and comfort items, also known as "ditty bags," for Allied soldiers towards the tail end of the war, circa 1945.[21]

Serapia recalled with fondness the simple gestures and passing signs of affection her future husband of over seventy years made towards her at the Army of-

---

[21] Tessie Jayme, "Red Cross in Manila," *Black Clouds in Manila*, Last Accessed August 26th, 2018, http://blackcloudsinmanila.com/Red-Cross.php.

fice building: "I would be writing at an office desk in a warehouse.... I would look at him and he would look at me. I would go home, and he [future husband] would give me a package [USAFFE rations]. He wasn't allowed to do that, to give those away, but he would do that to make us [get] to know each other. Soon, he askd my mother's permission to marry me and we got married in my little town."[22]

Serapia and Ricardo pose for their marriage licence, circa 1945, courtesy of the Aremas Family, Personal Collection.

---

[22] Sherry Aremas (World War II Philippine Guerrilla, Salinas *manang* pre-1965 generation), interviewed by Stacey Salinas, April 2018.

Within months of knowing one another, the migrant farm worker turned Supply Sergeant, and the *guerrillera* turned military clerk, were married on December 3, 1945, four months after the Japanese were defeated in the Philippines Campaign. Later, Ricardo would help fund Serapia's endeavors as a licensed fashion designer and seamstress at Samson's Fashion College of Manila. He did this while also putting together his and his wife's papers to leave for the United States, finding a new job to support his new family, and collecting enough capital to settle in California.

After graduation, Serapia and her husband were reunited. Together they took the daring voyage to the United States onboard the USS Meigs, a vessel once used as a transfer ship for troops during the war. Serapia's husband had served in the USAFFE and thus, under the Nationality Act of 1940, which allowed Filipinos who served in American uniform to become U.S. citizens, his citizenship status changed from "alien" to naturalized Filipino American.[23] His citizenship status helped Serapia remain united with her husband and seek a new life abroad. Through the ratification of

---

[23] Truman would abruptly deny the naturalization of many Filipino guerrillas, scouts, and those in both the regular and irregular units through the Veterans Rescission Acts of 1946. The discussion of compensation and follow up on honoring the sacrifices of all Filipino World War II veterans and granting them previous promises of American citizenship in 1990, and again in 2009. Deenesh Sohoni & Amin Vafa, "The Fight to Be American: Military Naturalization, and Asian Citizenship," *Asian American Law Journal*, Vol. 17 Article 4 (January 2010): 146.

the War Brides Act of 1947, 118,000 Filipina/o spouses and children, including Serapia, would be able to travel with their spouses or family to the United States and become naturalized American citizens.[24]

The happy couple settled in Salinas, California, a major agrarian hub for Filipino immigrant labor since the 1920s. They had a modest start, establishing their first home within Salinas' farming labor camps by 1947. Ricardo continued to labor in the lettuce fields as an irrigations expert for three years before going to work at Fort Ord. Serapia used her degree as a professional seamstress, sewing traditional Filipiniana gowns for the local Filipina wives and families in the area for special Filipino occasions and get-togethers, along with fulfilling other miscellaneous requests from the Filipino American community. Serapia's fervent and driven personality that helped her through the war also helped her to become a successful jack-of-all-trades career woman in Salinas. During the early years of their marriage, Serapia would support their little house and home they shared with other migrant labor farming families in the labor camps of Salinas through her various incomes. Although Serapia would come to define her status as a housewife, she continued to utilize and hire out many of her other skills. She became a professional cake decorator and beautician, with certificates for all her credentials to boot.

---

[24] Ronald H. Bayor, *Multicultural America: An Encyclopedia of the Newest Americans* (Santa Barbara: ABC-CLIO LLC., 2011), 714.

Serapia, upon arriving in the United States, began going by the name "Sherry." This was a split second change suggested by her husband-to-be (Serapia, he determined, might be too difficult for Americans to pronounce let alone sign) at the Army office that settled the legal work of their marriage. She also volunteered for the Filipino Women's Club of Salinas (one of the oldest Filipino organizations established in 1930), serving as an essential dress designer and seamstress of traditional women's wear for women's benefits, galas, and fundraising events.

Serapia's new life in the United States was symbolized by a multitude of roles, risky economic ventures, and cultural change. But she met those challenges head-on, and in the process, raised a young family, cultivated the Filipino American and Asian American communities of the Central Coast through her volunteer and auxiliary work, and became a woman representative of a new postwar age: a first generation Asian American woman with a multi-faceted professional persona, a community influencer, and an ever-multi-tasking mother and homemaker with a courageous World War II veteran *guerrillera* background.

Currently, in her late nineties, Serapia continues to support her Filipino American community as one of the oldest members of the Filipino Women's Club. Both she and her daughter, Susan Aremas (a devoted and retired school teacher), continue to operate and oversee scholarship fundraising for local Filipina/o

American Salinas youths and the monthly Filipino Women's Club meetings.

Lourdes Evangelista-Castro

Photographed above is Lourdes Castro, who at the age of eighteen served as a front line responder and medic.[25]

Even after the war, Filipina American veterans that arrived in the United States, like Serapia, remained driven in their endeavors to protect the interests and heritage of their ethnic communities. Lourdes Evangelista--Castro was also one such neighbor and community leader who found herself self-aggrandized by her *guerrillera* personality to continue serving her Fil--Am neighborhood and fellow veterans. Like Serapia who volunteers for

---

[25] Ben Menor & Marissa Castro Otto, "Lourdes Castro: The Story of a Rare and Great Hero," *Inquirer.Net*, Last Modified December 14th, 2011, Last Accessed December 19th, 2018,
https://globalnation.inquirer.net/20861/lourdes-castro-1926-2011-the-story-of-a-rare-and-great-hero.

Filipina/o led neighborhood organizations, Lourdes also volunteered in San Jose's Fil-am hub particularly at the Filipino Siquig Northside Community Center. There she preserved Filipino-American culture and helped to maintain an inviting and warm environment for first and second generation Asian American families in the San Jose area. Evidence of Lourdes' impact is in how she is remembered fondly by her community and family. Her daughter, Marisa Otto, described her "as a highly devoted mother and a grandmother and she was a trailblazer."[26] Other veterans who worked with her like Nolasco Mapalad described her as "very cooperative... helpful to her colleagues in explaining page by page veteran's benefits."[27] Such acts of commitment in protecting and invigorating the collectivity of one's hometown signal a common trend found amongst humble veteran heroes like Serapia represented.

Lourdes' post-war community building career was just as rich and impactful as her time as a guerrilla. At the age of eighteen, Lourdes Evangelista-Castro was inducted into the US Army for her bravery and courage undermining the Japanese and rescuing Filipino and American soldiers on the front lines. Lourdes brought multiple skill sets essential to war to the liberation front,

---

[26] Henni Espinosa, "Pinay War Veteran Dies Fighting for Justice," *ABS-CBN News*, Last Modified December 28th, 2011, Last Accessed December 31st, 2018.

[27] Espinosa, "Pinay War Veteran Dies Fighting for Justice."

being an experienced first responder medic, intelligence courier, and soldier.[28] As a guerrilla working for the Philippine Commonwealth Army and its Medical Corps, Lourdes pulled injured American and Filipino soldiers out of harm's way to tend to their wounds and participated in the famous liberation of the POW concentration camp of Los Banos. Because of her valiant efforts, she was inducted into the US Army; one of only two Filipinas during the war to officially be granted that honor.

After the war, Lourdes continued pursuing her passions for medicine. She would go on to receive both a bachelors and masters in Pharmacy, eventually working as a pharmacist at Fort Bonifacio (formerly known as Fort McKinley), what is now the headquarters of the Philippine Army in Metro Manila. Lourdes would marry, raise a family, build and run her own pharmacy business, and eventually become president of the Nueva Ecija Pharmaceutical Association.

In 1986, Lourdes and her family immigrated and settled in San Jose, California. It was there that she reclaimed her vigor and passion as a *guerrillera*: pursuing the reinstatement of all Filipina/o World War II veterans' benefits and their rights as neglected war heroes. Lourdes was one of the fortunate few who did

---

[28] Ysa Singson, "4 Empowering Pinay Warriors You Should Know: Not Your Stereotypical Maria Clara," *Cosmopolitan.ph*, Last Modified September 11th, 2016, Last Accessed December 23rd, 2018, https://www.cosmo.ph/lifestyle/empowering-pinay-warriors-filipiknow-a00177-20160912.

receive full benefits, including a pension granted to war veterans. She, just as she did as a wartime guerilla, continued to look out for her fellow Filipina/o comrades who served. She spoke on behalf of Filipina/o veterans as a council member who served on the Filipino American Community Development Council Inc. and became a founding member of the American Legion Northside Post 858, based in San Jose, where most of the members are Filipino veterans.[29]

On December 3rd, 2011, Lourdes passed away at the age of 85. Her legacy and historical narrative portray her as a hardworking woman of many talents and skills. Indeed, she was a pharmacist, businesswoman, community organizer and leader, civil rights activist, and World War II veteran. Her largest contribution to her countrymen and women—re-opening the conversation of Filipinos' veterans' status and recognition—continues to be an uphill battle. The lack of Asian ethnic groups' inclusion in World War II narratives mark the inherent racial, postcolonial, and political biases found in mainstream western and world histories of the war. Stories like Lourdes' are difficult to locate and bring to the surface, particularly because narratives like her's are remembered and searched for only by those communities that empathize and relate to wom-

---

[29] Henni Espinosa, "Pinay War Veteran Dies Fighting for Justice," *ABS-CBN.News*, Last Modified December 28th, 2011, Last Accessed December 26th, 2018, https://news.abs-cbn.com/global-filipino/12/27/11/pinay-war-veteran-dies-fighting-justice.

en of color like Lourdes Castro in the first place. Despite these obstacles towards broader recognition for women like Lourdes, her experiences as a woman-hero, her successful career, and her civil rights activism challenge the racially prejudiced taint associated with immigrant peoples of color. Above all, Lourdes' accomplishments expand the breadth and scope of immigrant and labor history to include transnational women of color veterans.

Pinay guerrilleras' actions and stations, regardless of how they understood their positions in the resistance, served as the seedlings that allowed for the underground resistance to carry on and find hope. Even for those hands who had little to no socio-economic means of political power—as Filipina women did before, during, and after the war—their experiences and contributions still provided lay people with the hope that one's limited station held merit and a means for more. These women lived very private lives, never speaking of their wartime exploits, focusing their post-war energies instead on supporting and raising their families. Although their wartime achievements displayed heroism that challenged gender conventions, many of these women found their future narratives bound yet again to serve their families. As a consequence, many of these women's heroic experiences became subsumed by their humble dedication to their families, and thus, they were rarely acknowledged or discussed until recently, thanks to President Barack Obama's administration.

One of President Obama's goals was to "right" long overdue obligations to historically marginalized peoples both on a domestic and international scale. For example, the American Recovery and Reinvestment Act of 2009 created the World War II Filipino Veterans Equity Compensation Fund. This fund represented a lump-sum payment to eligible Filipino World War II veterans. President Obama's White House Initiative on AAPIs (Asian American Pacific Islanders) worked with Filipino veterans to allow for fair, efficient processing, and review of applications to support awards to as many veterans as possible. As of 2016, a total of 42,755 applications were processed with over $225 million having been paid out.[30]

The World War II Filipino Veterans Equity Compensation Fund represents one of the first steps towards recognizing and including Filipina/o contributions to both American history and World War II narratives. The *guerrillera* veterans covered in this chapter point to the many gaps in such popular histories. These women's immigrant histories may appear, at first glance, to be isolated and only mentioned by the communities they lived and served in. But, in reality,

---

[30] Billy Dec, "Honoring Filipino WWII Veterans this Filipino American History Month," *The White House: President Barack Obama,* Last Modified October 3rd, 2016, Last Accessed December 24th, 2018, https://obamawhitehouse.archives.gov/blog/2016/10/03/honoring-filipino-wwii-veterans-filipino-american-history-month.

their compassion and dedication to serve their families and local communities in quieter capacities—towards what others might consider less extraordinary ends—reveals how their days as *guerrilleras* granted them a certain kind of resilience. These "ordinary" women created new lives in the United States, focused on their families, and aimed for careers that supported a simple, self-effacing livelihood for themselves, their families, and their own Asian American communities. Their selflessness and devotion to such "modest" priorities and ability to persevere in any environment or career they chose, taken together with their exceptional wartime feats, reveals that they too are heroes, despite humble appearances.

Chapter 5

The Legacy of the
Asian Woman Soldier

MacArthur's famous landing on the island of Leyte in October of 1944 launched another wave of guerrilla warfare that forced the surrender of the Imperial Japanese Army. The Battle of Manila began in February of 1945 and would continue for a month, causing many Allied, Japanese, and civilian casualties in the capital.[1] After the American and Philippine troops reclaimed Manila, MacArthur deemed the Philippines liberated, leaving the final task of eliminating the last stands of Japanese resistance to the guerrillas. Huk commanders like Simeona Punsalan and Liwayway were tasked with rooting out the last of the Japanese stragglers in Central Luzon. The fighting between remaining individual enemy units and Philippine guerrilla troops continued until the Japanese branch in the mountain region of Northern Luzon officially surrendered in August 1945.

---

[1] James M. Scott, Rampage: MacArthur, Yamashita, and the Battle of Manila (W.W. Norton & Company, 2018), Part II, Chapter 6.

For most resistance fighters the end of the Japanese occupation marked the end of their guerilla career. Some continued to fight against the new Philippine government, which in many ways continued the landed bureaucracies and social caste systems previously implemented by both the Spanish and American occupations. Huk women like Simeona Punsalan, Liwayway, and Mariano-Pomeroy would go underground with their husbands, fighting for the rights and inclusion of peasant farmers, the landless laborers, and those Filipinas/os denied veterans' benefits. In contrast, other guerrillas considered their mission accomplished when the Japanese signed their official surrender in 1945.

Public Memory and Remembering the Filipina War Hero

The Philippine Resistance reflected the cultural and socio-economic diversity of the Philippine Islands. From socialist peasant farmers, middle school teachers, ROTC youths, to Moro (Philippine Muslim) warriors, the range and inclusivity of the men and women who participated in the struggle against the Japanese Imperial Army was incredible. Women guerrilla fighters especially made major contributions to the liberation of the Philippines, but unfortunately, similar to other ethnic minority guerrilla fighters, have received less acknowledgment and discussion in World War II histories of the Pacific Theater.

During the early half of the twentieth century, the Philippines witnessed few advances in women's rights. But with the threat of war and the encroachment of the Japanese Imperial Army upon the Philippine Islands, the patriarchal and religiously conservative culture of the Philippines could not afford to maintain its traditional gender hierarchy. The grassroots resistance drew in the patriotic fervor of many Filipinas, who saw the guerrilla resistance as an opportunity to liberate their homeland as well as prove the capabilities of their sex. Their guerrilla efforts proved women were more than capable of taking on numerous roles: soldiers, leaders, activists, journalists, nurses, doctors, spies, and dedicated patriots. Filipina guerrillas proved to be a vital aspect of both soldiering and reconnaissance missions, allowing for the Allies to gain an opportunity to retake the Philippines.

Historians estimate that, for every ten male guerrillas, one Filipina guerrilla served in the underground resistance.[2] Over 260,000 male Filipino guerrillas served the resistance effort.[3] The fact that only male guerrillas have been counted reflects how Filipinas in

---

[2] Vina Lanzona, *Amazons of the Huk Rebellion: Gender, Sex, and Revolution in the Philippines* (University of Wisconsin Press, 2009), 7.

[3] Nicholas Trajano Molnar, American Mestizos, *The Philippines, and the Malleability of Race: 1898-1961* (University of Missouri Press, 2017), 126.

wartime history has been neglected, either being ignored or not counted as officially serving, despite female guerrilla populations representing possibly more than 10% of the guerrilla resistance. These statistics, along with the little surviving resources on Filipina guerrilla efforts, brings to light the missing narratives of a traditionally American-centered history on the liberation of the Philippines of World War II. The wartime experiences of women of color in the Pacific highlights the various contributions, struggles, and cultural diversity that aided and represented the Allied front of the Pacific.

Filipina guerrillas, like their male peers, were aware of the risks and sacrifices they made in their efforts to push the Japanese Imperial Army out of the Philippines. One of the added fears and risks that all Filipinas shared, which their male peers did not, was the threat of rape and being forcibly used as comfort women (sex slaves) for the Japanese Imperial Army. Despite the risks of death, torture, and rape, the Filipina guerrillas of the Philippine Resistance persevered, representing the hardy and selfless cause of both liberations from the Japanese imperial regime and progress towards women's rights in Southeast Asia.

The invasion and occupation of the Philippines by the Japanese Imperial Army would breed another generation of Filipina *guerrilleras*, armed with both nationalist determination and soldierly stamina. The Allied surrender at Corregidor, the horrors of the Bataan Death March, and the Philippines' long history of female fighters culminated in leadership opportunities for empowered *pinays*, primarily because of their staunch resistance to enemy occupation throughout the duration of the war. And yet, despite the efforts and sacrifices of *pinay guerrilleras*, Asian women's roles in the war continue to be commonly depicted within the framework of traditional gender conventions: as nurses, caregivers, and motherly hands and faces lending their shoulder to the wounded allies. These portrayals of *guerrilleras*, rather than their efforts as leaders, fighters, and scouts, are far more prevalent in both the written histories and material culture produced during and after the war. But, as this book demonstrates, the roles of *pinay* insurgents were far more active and diverse than what American and Filipino films, wartime literature, and propaganda material have promoted within the last seventy-five years.

Popular movies released after the war portrayed Filipina women in the background and supporting roles. In both Filipino and American cinema, Filipinas were portrayed as either exotic love interests to the main characters, nurses, or village non-combatants or bystanders. In films like *An American Guerrilla in the Philippines*, released in 1950, the hero and leader of the resistance is an American soldier, Ensign Chuck Palmer, stranded in the Philippines following the Japanese invasion. He falls in love with a rich French woman married to a Filipino landowner, who later in the film becomes a guerrilla. Women resistance sympathizers portrayed in this film are seen as far more interested in love than war. Even worse, the film does not recognize Filipina/o actors in the credits, with the main "Filipino" protagonists not being ethnically Filipino; the role of the Filipino landowner was played by Spanish actor, Juan Torena, while the Leyte Filipino resistance fighter was played by American actor Tommy Cooke.[4] In the film, the Western Allies are front and center as the leaders and heroes of the resistance, not Filipinos, and certainly not Filipinas.

Postwar Filipino films were also guilty of portraying Filipinas in war as lovesick heroines, secondary to male protagonists. Film scholars have dubbed the late 1940s for Filipino cinema as the "Liberation" period.[5] These wartime films highlight the struggles of Filipinos, particularly as noble heroes of the resistance. Two films that capture the inclusion of women guerrillas are *Batalyon XIII* (1949) and *Guerilyera* (1946). In both films, *mestiza* actress, Carmen Rosales takes center stage. She herself was a *guerrilla* who on numerous occasions disguised herself as a man to avoid Japanese suspicion. She was a spy and sharpshooter guerrilla,

---

[4] IMDB, "Actor: Juan Torena," *IMDB.Com*, Last Accessed December 27th, 2018, https://www.imdb.com/name/nm0867944/.

[5] Danny Dolor, "Carmen Rosales as Guerilyera," Last Modified June 14th, 2014, Last Accessed December 27th, 2018, https://www.pressreader.com/philippines/the-philippine-star/20150614/282402693010462.

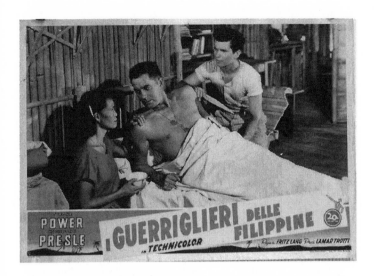

In the movie poster shown above, the Filipina actress who is not credited in the film, is seen as a silent villager, a pseudo medical aide, whose role falls into the part of the broad Philippine landscape. She is a villager, a nurse, but not one who is deemed essential or part of the resistance on a militant level.[6]

driven by the murder of her husband by the Japanese at the start of the war.[7] In these films, she plays a guerrilla fighter, modeled after her own experiences. She brandishes guns, has a bright and spunky personality, and is filmed in a way that does not subordinate her to her male comrades. But alas, she too was a woman who

---

[6] IMDB, "American Guerrilla In the Philippines," *IMDB.Com*, https://www.imdb.com/title/tt0042195/?ref_=ttfc_fc_tt.
[7] Marichu Maceda, "Carmen Rosales: The Genuine Superstar," *PhilStar Global*, Last Modified MArch 6th, 2005, Last Accessed December 27th, 2018, https://www.philstar.com/entertainment/2005/03/06/269261/carmen-rosales-genuine-superstar.

Sampaguita Pictures movie posters of *Guerilyera* (1946)
starring a *guerrillera* herself, Carmen Rosales as the main
actor and protagonist.[8]

gave into more romantic desires, being portrayed as a
supportive lover as much as she was a soldier.

Rosales' films during the "Liberation" era reflect the
earliest public memories and sentiments about female
guerrillas during the war. Although Rosales portrayed
women fighters as independent, adept with weapons,
and qualified in strategizing and espionage, her characters were still susceptible to more "feminine" vir-

---

[8] Video 48, "Carmen Rosales," *Video 48: A Virtual Online Library and
Archive On Philippine Cinema*, Last Modified April 30th 2008, Last Accessed December 27th, 2018, http://video48.blogspot.com/search?q=
Carmen+Rosales. Danny Dolor, "Carmen Rosales as Guerilyera," Last
Modified June 14th, 2014, Last Accessed December 27th, 2018,
https://www.pressreader.com/philippines/the-philippine-star/
20150614/282402693010462.

tues, with her films highlighting her *mestiza* beauty and her love interests.

Another Filipino film, *Victory Joe* (1946), also hails from the same "Liberation" cinema era that leaves a rather bland portrayal of Filipinas affected by the war. *Mestiza* actress Norma Blancaflor plays the role of a country girl named Rosie mourning the loss of her soldier boyfriend who, early in the film, is believed to have died in battle. She soon becomes the object of affection of an American soldier, played by Art Cantrell. Despite the stigma attached to Filipinas who entertain or date American officers, typically seen as women with "loose" morals, Rosie returns the officer's affections thinking that this new romance will help her to overcome the loss of her previous lover. As the war comes to a close and the American troops receive their discharge papers to return to the United States, Rosie is torn up emotionally yet again as her Filipino soldier, played by Rogelio De La Rosa, surprisingly returns hoping to start afresh with Rosie in the countryside.

Throughout the film, Blancaflor's character, in essence, represents a woman in a war driven only by her emotions. Among the other recurrent themes associated with the afflicted wartorn Filipina that the character Rosie fulfills, another gendered motif that is most visible is how she is defined by her romantic relationships with men. Her sole role in the war, unfortunately, is as a figure of emotional support for her lovers on the front lines. It is the men in the film whose actions and decisions move the story along. Both soldiers force Rosie to make a choice between which lover she will take and it is the two soldiers in the end who jointly, and without hard feelings, decide which man is better suited for Rosie; the Filipino veteran Eduardo.[9] Rosie's personality and absent decision making thus play into the classical interpretation of Philippine gender conventions of the period; that even in war duress, women like Rosie were relegated to the roles of a civilian bystander who could only serve in the war as a supportive doting partner.

The film production depicting Colonel Yay Panlilio's war experience and biography, *The Crucible*, played on similar tropes of Filipina femininity. The film, *Cry Freedom* (1959), starred another *mestiza* actress, Rosa Rosal, as Colonel Yay Panlilio.[10] The film portrayal of Panlilio is also guilty of emphasizing and elevating Rosa's/Panlilio's *mestiza* attributes, and also portrayed Rosa's character, like Panlilio's wartime memoir, as more of a love interest to Colonel Agustin (played by Pancho Magalona), rather than a military

---

[9] Rogelio De La Rosa & Norma Blancaflor, *Victory Joe*, directed by Manuel Silos. LVN Pictures, Metro Manila, 1946.

[10] *Cry Freedom*, film, 1959, 1hr & 33 minutes. Lamberto V. Avellana, director. Actors: Pancho Magalona, Rosa Rosal. Film Summary: A man and a woman fight for the freedom of their country – Marking with his gun – Yay with her typewriter. Thrown together by a cause greater than either of them they share the suffering of the flesh and the spirit among the country's guerrilla fighters. They emerge, out of the crucible of war, heroes-and lovers. IMDB "Cry Freedom," *IMDB.Com,* Last Accessed December 27th, 2018, https://www.imdb.com/title/tt0054771/plotsummary?ref_=tt_ov_pl.

guerrilla leader in her own right. Their love affair is central to the film, with Panlilio's character's charm and beauty being directly associated with her romantic relationship, rather than with her leadership role in the Marking's Guerrilla unit. In nearly every scene, Panlilio is depicted more as an attachment to the central figure of the Marking Guerrilla troops, Colonel Agustin, rather than as a free-thinking woman who stood on her own as a soldier.

Within the last decade, the Obama Administration sought to challenge the conservative and gendered narrative of the Pacific Theater's guerrilla history. Indeed, the Filipino Veterans Equity Compensation Fund currently recognizes female guerrillas for their noble participation and activity—given that such individuals or their family can prove their participation with the proper legal paperwork. For those women who contributed to the resistance's cause, finding the resources, time, and additional energy to put together one's papers, even after the war, was a grueling task. Many guerrillas, particularly those in more remote regions, such as the indigenous peoples like the *Aetas,* continue to find it nearly impossible to secure proof (which requires personal funding for lawyers to oversee their request) of their role in the war.[11]

---

[11] Tonette Orejas, "Pension Elusive for Aeta Guerrillas," *Inquirer.Net,* Last Modified March 2nd, 2014, Last Accessed December 28th, 2018, https://newsinfo.inquirer.net/769917/pension-elusive-for-aeta-guerrillas.

The 1959 Banaue Films film posters of the movie *Cry Freedom*. The subheadings and images chosen for the popular movie posters depict Panlilio as more of a romantic interest rather than a *guerrillera* at first glance.[12]

---

[12] Danny Dolore, "Cry Freedom: Love & War," *Philippine Star*, Last Modified April 9th, 2016, Last Accessed December 23rf, 2018, https://www.philstar.com/entertainment/2016/04/09/1571156/cry-freedom-love-war. Video 48, "THE FIFTIES # 618: PANCHO MAGALONA AND ROSA ROSAL IN LAMBERTO V. AVELLANA'S "CRY FREEDOM" (1959)," *Video48: A Virtual Online Library and Archive of Philippine Cinema*, Last Modified April 22nd, 2014, Last Accessed December 27h, 2018, http://video48.blogspot.com/2014/04/the-fifties-618-pancho-magalona-and.html.

Gendered expectations serve to further prevent *pinay* guerrillas of any opportunity to successfully file for their benefits. If a woman served as a nurse or support staff to the guerrillas, or even housed or fed the guerrillas, does she count as an official guerrilla, even if she did not physically fight the Japanese herself? What if she was a pledged guerrilla combatant like Captain Diaz was in Yay Panlilio's memoir, but the only proof that her family could rely on to apply for family veteran's benefits were scattered accounts of other soldiers' narratives? Such examples speak directly to the gendered cultural biases that women of color face, as well as their continual struggle against intersectional (gender, racial, class, nationality, citizenship, labor-based) prejudices.

The *guerrillera* generation is currently reaching their late nineties and early hundreds, and their stories will soon be forgotten if efforts to preserve their histories continue to be hindered by dominating male-centered narratives tinged with discriminative gender tones and overly broad interpretations of women's roles and agency throughout the war. As exemplified by *guerrilleras* like Serapia Aremas and Lourdes Castro, women's roles on the front lines of the liberation front are evidence of female heroes re-defining the hypermasculinized space of the Pacific Theater.

Despite *guerrillera* efforts and their experiences, many saw their roles as inconsequential, painting themselves as supporting characters, middle (wo)men simply trying to do the right thing. Or, in other case studies, like that of Serapia Aremas, they saw themselves merely as volunteers who intently listened and followed orders coming down from the real "center of the action," their male captains or peers. In truth, the war would transform these women, making them just as impactful as the male guerrillas and captains who led them. By stepping into the role of liberator, *guerrilleras* challenged universal gender conventions and racialized colonial hierarchies. They liberated their home barrios and their country from the Japanese occupation. Their dedication to the front lines reveals just how capable *all* Philippine citizens were of self-government and of establishing political agendas that were in their best interests. Guerrilla Huks established their own small body politics through which common people could manage their own resources and commerce resources, without any imperialist entity, like Spain or the United States, interfering.

But their participation in the war, unbeknownst to them, further influenced their actions and unrelenting character in the postwar era. It is true that they might have followed the traditional outlook expected for Filipinas—they married and established their own house and future for their families. Nonetheless, these women were still taking a risk, immigrating and rearing their children in a foreign place like the United States during a time where xenophobia and racial prejudices ran rampant. Their bravery earned them their economic independence postwar when American values reverted back to emphasizing women's roles as homemakers during the Cold War. In such an environment, even the act of wanting and pursuing an education in the United States as a full-time mother in a highly racialized environment was risky. But for these former *guerrilleras*, their wartime attitude stuck with them, with their achievements going on to inspire the next generation of Filipinas and Filipina Americans to constantly strive to be better.

Conclusion

FILIPINO GUERRILLAS

BY GREG. S. SAN DIEGO

We did not sleep—we who refused to die,
Nor shirked to face war on our native ground;
We did not weep, but stood against the cry
Of madmen bent on spreading griefs around.

We weren't afraid: fear was not in our blood.
We only knew that freedom must be strong.
Else all would be but worthless gifts of God
And life, a drab and lonely thing of song.

To face the common foe, to hope and wait,
Then jump at some opportune time to kill;
To blast the heart of madness out of hate
And write our tale of brav'ry on the hill—

We are the men who fought and waited long,
For we believed that freedom must be strong.

A poem by a Filipino guerrilla describing their patriotic zeal and dedication to the Philippines' liberation describing the guerrillas as only a male fighting force, circa 1945.[1]

---

[1] Greg S. San Diego, "Filipino Guerrillas," *The Philippines Mail*, February 1945, Steinbeck Public Library, Salinas.

When reading World War II narratives such as *Men of Destiny: The American and Filipino Guerrillas During the Japanese Occupation of the Philippines*, the Filipina guerrilla presence is blatantly absent. Despite the immense depth and variety that World War II literature and historiography offers, the people of color, particularly women of color in all theaters of the war, are glazed over. Women portrayed in wartime literature are primarily understood as passive, supporting figures, labeled as wives, cooks, and nurses for resistance fighters, or, more commonly, depicted as victims or casualties of war. The experiences of American female spies, military wives and daughters, and nurses, like those of the Angels of Bataan highlighted in Elizabeth Norman's work *We Band of Angels: The Untold Story of the American Women Trapped on Bataan*, have only recently come to light.

Norman's historical piece conveys the physical and psychological turmoil American nurses felt as they tried to make do with what little resources they had to heal both the Filipino and American soldiers in the tunnels of Corregidor under their care. After the fall of Corregidor, the American and Filipino nurses of Bataan were captured by the Imperial Japanese Army. Though they were not forced to walk the Bataan Death March, they were forced into the POW internment camps of Santo Tomas and Los Banos. The American nurses continued to help the soldiers at the camps with what little resources they were given by the Japanese, while they themselves were also under physical duress, contracting scurvy and pellagra.

The liberation of the camps in 1945 by the combined efforts of the Allied troops and Philippine guerrillas meant that the American nurses could finally go home. But, as Norman describes from the interviews conducted with twenty veteran nurses in their late eighties, the nurses were not to be given distinguished recognition for their sacrifices and courage by the American Army. Rather, upon returning home, the women were asked questions that were gender prejudiced and insensitive, regarding how they felt about contemporary fashion, or if they were raped, in other words, nothing along the lines of their devotion to their country and profession.[2]

Norman's *We Band of Angels* (1999) and Theresa Kaminski's *Prisoners in Paradise: American Women in the Wartime South Pacific* (2000), are some of the few pieces of historical literature that investigates and adds to women's history in the Pacific Theater. Kaminski's more recent book, *Angels of the Underground: The American Women Who Resisted the Japanese In the Philippines in World War II* (2016), expands the discussion of the female participants of the resistance, but mainly as the title suggests, from the American women's perspectives. And although Kaminski is keen to

---

[2] Elizabeth M. Norman, *We Band of Angels: The Untold Story of the American Women Trapped on Bataan* (New York: Random House Trade Paperback, 2013), 226.

take note of the *mestiza* Filipina guerrillas or collaborators such as Yay Panlilio and Florence Ebersole, the presence, scope, and broader perspective of the Filipina guerrilla is unevenly distributed, or minimal.[3] Indeed, Norman and Kaminski's works provide another page to the remarkable vanguard moments in women's world history by highlighting American women's wartime biographies. Yet, even so, the experiences of Filipina guerrillas, nurses, civilians, and mothers—the women of color in the Pacific—remain scattered, voiceless, invisible, and absent.

Filipina guerrillas came from all walks of life. Some were communist party members like Commander Liwayway, who hoped to reshape the postwar Philippines into a more egalitarian state. Others were film actresses like Carmen Rosales, who became further incensed and galvanized to join the resistance after her husband's death at the hands of the Imperial Japanese Army. Filipina guerrilla fighters, despite their diverse backgrounds, had a common goal: to liberate their nation from Japanese occupation, secure the Philippine peoples' civil rights and independence, and restore the islands they called home. In their fight for liberation, these Filipina warriors showcased the underlying resilience and overwhelming untapped potential wo-

---

[3] Theresa Kaminski, *Angels of the Underground: The American Women Who Resisted the Japanese In the Philippines in World War II* (New York: Oxford University Press, 2016), 29, 178, 230, 341.

men of color had as military, political, and educational leaders, regardless of class, race, religion, and sex.

Guerrilleras fought on multiple fronts: against gender and racial prejudices, the Japanese occupation, and intra-ethnic gender politics. Many *guerrilleras* would never fully be recognized for their efforts in the Pacific Theater, which has perpetuated the imagery of the underground resistance as a male-dominated and hyper-masculine wartime environment. The hurdles that *guerrilleras* had to overcome to establish their own niche as soldiers and military and community leaders were directly influenced and made more insurmountable by the limitations of traditional gender and Filipino cultural norms. Filipinas found themselves delegated to the caregiver and supporting roles. Those Filipinas who sought to participate on the battlefield, or in strategic and leadership positions, were doubly questioned and challenged by male superiors who continuously tried to maintain gendered relationships of power, even in extreme wartime climates.

By maintaining gender norms in camps, civilian settings, and familial households, Filipino resistance and military leaders could still hold onto one strong aspect of Filipino cultural normalities—patriarchal dominance—in the face of Japanese occupation.

The *guerrilleras* of World War II—their military leadership, espionage, love of their country, and culture—harken back to the Filipina warrior narrative exemplified first by the mighty Princess Urduja. But, like Urduja, whose history transformed into folklore and myth, so too did the contributions and faces of the female resistance fighters of the Philippines blur into distinct and narrow categories of the preferred traditional type of heroine. Those women whose sacrifices, personalities, social caste, or appearance did not align with the cookie cutter narrative of the imagined Filipina amazon, were re-imagined as having more supportive roles in the war. Other *guerrilleras*, who did not partake in the postwar politics of the new Philippine Republic or military have, unfortunately, been nearly forgotten. Their stories continue to fall through the cracks of recently established fields of scholarship, like women's history, world history, and immigrant labor/migration history.

Women resistance fighters in this book have, in one way or another, been affected by the gender bias that so often marginalizes the efforts of women in war. Indeed, as we have seen, many *guerrilleras* were characterized as overly emotional, romantic, and simpler compared to their male counterparts. As the biased descriptions of Yay Panlilio's contributions reveal, they supposedly gave into girlish whims and the charms of male soldiers. Other women, like the Huk commander Culala (Dayang-Dayang), was remembered as a self-involved commander who gave in too easily to selfish desires and was far too aggressive, selfish, and self-aggrandizing, leading to a terrible and shameful execution. The "ordinary" Filipina resistance soldiers, who chose to make the daring trek across the Pacific, became more defined by their career as homemakers rather than as *guerrilleras*. Like other women who were part of the second wave of Asian immigration patterns, they became known as perpetually foreign, loyal, and submissive "War Bride[s]."[4]

Filipina resistance fighters were forced to stay true to traditional forms of gender etiquette whilst operating as guerrillas. Even in extreme environments, women who wanted to participate in the war felt compelled to act as caregivers rather than fighters. Even when they did fight alongside men, they still had to act as mothers and sisters more than they would have liked to. Due to the gender hierarchy that defined the Philippines, *guerrilleras* were consistently criticized for their desire to fight, let alone be seen on the ground amongst men, and were even given harsh court marshalls and sentences for speaking out against men they outranked, as exemplified by Commander Culala. Despite these setbacks, the Filipina guerrilla stories that survive are a remarkable testament to the women of color who defied such gendered odds and survived captivity, brutal beatings, and rape, and who conti-

---

[4] Maddalena Marinari, Madeline Hsu, Maria Cristina Garcia ed, *A Nation of Immigrants Reconsidered: US Society in an Age of Restriction, 1924--1965* (University of Illinois Press, 2018), "Chapter 11: Japanese War Brides and the Normalization of Family Unification After World War II."

nued to advocate for the recognition of Filipinas and their role in ending the Japanese occupation.

Pinay veterans could be described in a number of ways, including as confidently aggressive, soft, charismatic, quick-thinking, posh, peasant farmers, socialists, six-foot amazons, lepers, mothers, soldiers, mixed race, activists, and more. Whichever description used to memorialize these women, *guerrilleras* in one way or another reshaped gender conventions on their own terms, both during the upheaval of war and period that followed. They, along with countless other inspired Filipinas, would continue using their strength to oversee the newly independent Philippines during the Cold War. The hardy Huk women, like the lipstick toting Commander Liwayway and Commander Simeona Punsalan, would continue the good fight for the inclusion of peasant farmers, laborers, and fair representation of Huk-communist veterans well into the late twentieth century. Others immigrated to the United States, hoping to create a new life for themselves and their families as mothers and career women. Regardless of the paths these women took in their later years, their confidence, stamina, and determination forged new opportunities and futures for women of color on a global scale.

For more information regarding the Pacific Theater, the guerrilla resistance in the Philippines, and more remarkable first hand accounts of other guerrilleras who served in the Pacific Theater, please look into the Pacific Atrocities Education's other publications:

Stacey Anne Baterina Salinas & Klytie Xu, *Philippines' Resistance: The Last Allied Stronghold in the Pacific.* Pacific Atrocities Education, 2017.

Derek Pua, Danielle Dybbro, & Alistair Rogers, *Unit 731: The Forgotten Auschwitz.* Pacific Atrocities Education, 2018.

Paulina Hernandez, Julie Porter, & Christopher Sayas. *Cannibalism Culture: The Bushido Horror In World War II.* Pacific Atrocities Education, 2018.

Jenny Chan & Derek Pua. *Three Years, Eight Months: The Japanese Occupation of Hong Kong.* Pacific Atrocities Education, 2017.

Mei Mei Chun-Moy, Sally Ma, Mark Witzke. *Fall of Singapore: The Undefeatable British Fortress Conquered.* Pacific Atrocities Education, 2017.

Works Cited

Books

Arrizon, Alicia. *Queering Mestizaje: Transculturation and Performance*. Ann Arbor: University of Michigan Press, 2009.

Atwood, Kathryn J. *Women Heroes of World War II: The Pacific Theater, 15 Stories of Resistance, Rescue, Sabotage, and Survival*. Chicago: Chicago Review Press Incorporated, 2017.

Bayor, Ronald H. *Multicultural America: An Encyclopedia of the Newest Americans*. Santa Barbara: ABC-CLIO LLC., 2011.

Bennett, Tom. *World War II Wrecks of the Philippines: WWII Shipwrecks of the Philippines*. Philippines: Happy Fish Publications, 2010.

Boyer, Robert H. *Sundays in Manila*. Quezon City: The University of the Philippines Press, 2010.

Buell, Thomas B., John H. Bradley, and Jack W. Dice, *The Second World War: Asia and the Pacific*. Singapore: Square One Publishers, 2002.

Dahl, Erik J. *Intelligence and Surprise Attack: Failure and Success from Pearl Harbor to 9/11 and Beyond*. Georgetown University Press, 2013.

Del Castillo y Tuazon, Antonio. *Princess Urduja, Queen of the Orient Seas: Before and After her Time in the Political Orbit of the Shri-vi-ja-ya and the Madjapahit Maritime Empire: a Pre-Hispanic History of the Philippines.* University of Michigan, 1998.

Chun, Clayton. *The Fall of the Philippines, 1941-1942.* Osprey Publishing, 2012.

Cuizon, Erma M. *Twilight in Misamis: Josefa Borromeo Capistrano's Guerrilla Days.* Cebu City: University of San Carlos Press, 2014.

Cruz, Denise. *Transpacific Femininities: The Making of the Modern Filipina.* Durham & London: Duke University Press, 2012.

Duka, Cecilio D. *Struggle for Freedom.* Manila: Rex Publishing, 2008.

Greenberger, Robert. *Snapshots in History: The Bataan Death March: World War II in the Pacific.* Mankato: Compass Point Books, 2009.

Henson, Maria Rosa. *Comfort Woman: A Filipina's Story of Prostitution and Slavery Under the Japanese Military.* London: Rowman & Littlefield, 2017.

Hing, Bill Ong. *Making and Remaking Asian America Through Immigration Policy: 1850-1990.* Stanford: Stanford University Press, 1993.

Ikehata, Setsuho & Ricardo Trota Jose. *The Philippines Under Japan: Occupation Policy and Reaction.* University of Hawaii Press, 1999.

Ingham, Travis. *Rendezvous By Submarine: The Story of Charles Parsons and the Guerrilla-Soldiers in the Philippines.* Los Angeles: The Bowsprit Press, 2018.

Ishida, Miki Y. *Toward Peace: War Responsibility, Postwar Compensation, and Peace Movements and Education in Japan.* New York: iUniverse, Inc., 2005.

Jacob, Frank. *Japanese War Crimes During World War II: Atrocity and Psychology of Collective Violence.* Santa Barbara: Frank Jacob, 2018.

Kaminski, Theresa. *Angels of the Underground: The American Women Who Resisted the Japanese in World War II.* New York: Oxford University Press, 2016.

Kaminski, Theresa. *Prisoners in Paradise: American Women in the Wartime South Pacific.* University Press of Kansas, 2000.

Keats, John. *They Fought Alone: A True Story of an American Hero.* Echo Point Books and Media, 2015.

Kim, Eileen Yujoo. *Korean Comfort Women: Political and Personal History Intertwined.* Berkeley: University of California Press, 1997.

Lansdale, Edward Geary. *In the Midst of Wars: An American's Mission to Southeast Asia.* New York: Fordham University Press, 1991.

Lanzona, Vina A. *Amazons of the Huk Rebellion: Gender, Sex, and Revolution in the Philippines.* Madison: University of Wisconsin Press, 2009.

Leary, William M. ed., *We Shall Return!: MacArthur's Commanders and the Defeat of Japan, 1942-1945.* Lexington: The University of Kentucky Press, 1988.

Lee, Ernesto. *World War II Philippines: A Boy's Tale of Survival.* Xlibris Corporation, 2010.

Li, Peter ed. *Japanese War Crimes.* New Brunswick: Routledge, 2017.

Maceda, Teresita Gimenez. *Bride of War: My Mother's World War II Memories.* Mandaluyong City: Anvil Publishing, 2011.

Maga, Timothy P. *Judgement at Tokyo: The Japanese War Crimes Trials.* Lexington: University of Press of Kentucky, 2001.

Marinari, Maddalena, Madeline Hsu, Maria Cristina Garcia ed. *A Nation of Immigrants Reconsidered: US Society in an Age of Restriction, 1924-1965.* University of Illinois Press, 2018.

Masato Kimura, Tosh Minohara ed. *Tumultuous Decade: Empire, Society, and Diplomacy in 1930s Japan.* Toronto: University of Toronto Press, 2013.

Masuda, Hiroshi. *MacArthur in Asia: The General and His Staff in the Philippines, Japan, and Korea.* London: Cornell University Press, 2009.

McCoy, Alfred W. *Policing America's Empire: The United States, The Philippines, and the Rise of the Surveillance State.* Madison: University of Wisconsin Press, 2009.

Mills, Scott. *Stranded in the Philippines: Professor Bell's Private War Against the Japanese.* Annapolis: Naval Institute Press, 2009.

Molnar, Nicholas Trajano. *American Mestizos, The Philippines, and the Malleability of Race: 1898-1961.* University of Missouri Press, 2017.

Montgomery, Ben. *Leper Spy: The Story of an Unlikely Hero of World War II.* Illinois: Chicago Review Press Incorporated, 2017.

Morton, Louis. *The War in the Pacific: Strategy and Command, the First Two Years.* Washington D.C.: Center of Military History United States Army, 2000.

Morton, Louis. *United States Army in World War II: The War in the Pacific – Fall of the Philippines*. Washington, DC: Office of the Chief of Military History, Department of the Army, 1953.

Murphy, Kevin C. *Inside the Bataan Death March: Defeat, Travail and Memory*. Jefferson: McFarland, 2014.

Nadal, Kevin L. *Filipino American Psychology: A Handbook of Theory, Research, and Clinical Practice*. Bloomington: Authorhouse, 2009.

Nalty, Bernard C. ed. *War in the Pacific: Pearl Harbor to Tokyo Bay, the Story of the Bitter Struggle in the Pacific Theater of World War II*. Norman: University of Oklahoma Press, 1999.

National Centennial Commission, *Sulong Pilipina! Sulong Pilipinas!: A Compilation of Filipino Women Centennial Awardees*. National Centennial Commission, Women Sector, 1999.

Norman, Elizabeth M. *We Band of Angels: The Untold Story of the American Women Trapped on Bataan*. New York: Random House Trade Paperback, 2013.

Nuval, Leonardo Q. *Remember Them Kindly: Some Filipinos During World War II*. Claretian Publications, 1996.

Panicello, Joseph Francis. *A Slow Moving Target: The LST of World War II*. Joseph Francis Panicello, 2001.

Panlilio, Yay. *The Crucible: An Autobiography by Colonel Yay, Filipina American Guerrilla*. New Brunswick: Rutgers University Press, 1950.

Perry, Mark. *The Most Dangerous Man in America: The Making of Douglas MacArthur*. New York: Basic Books, 2014.

Polette, Nancy. *P.O.W. Angel on Call: The True Story of an American Guerrilla Nurse in the Philippines During World War II.* Blessinks, 2013.

Poole, Peter A. *Politics and Society in Southeast Asia.* North Carolina: McFarland & Company, 2009.

Rodao, Florentine and Felice Noelle Rodriguez ed. *The Philippine Revolution of 1896: Ordinary Lives in Extraordinary Times.* Manila: Ateneo de Manila University Press, 2001.

Sinclair II, Major Peter T. *Men of Destiny: The American and Filipino Guerrillas During the Japanese Occupation of the Philippines.* Pickle Partners Publishing, 2015.

Sohoni, Deenesh & Amin Vafa. "The Fight to Be American: Military Naturalization, and Asian Citizenship." *Asian American Law Journal.* Vol. 17 Article 4 (January 2010): 119-151.

Spencer, Louise Reid. *Guerrilla Wife.* Pickle Partners Publishing, 2017.

Stetz, Margaret D. & Bonnie B. C. Oh ed. *Legacies of the Comfort Women of World War II.* New York: Routledge, 2015.

Tanaka, Toshiyuki. *Hidden Horrors: Japanese War Crimes in World War II.* Westview Press, 1996.

Triplet, William S. *In the Philippines and Okinawa: A Memoir, 1945-1948.* Columbia: University of Missouri Press, 2001.

Waines, Davis. *The Odyssey of Ibn Battuta: Uncommon Tales of a Medieval Adventurer.* New York: I.B. Tauris & Co, 2010.

Walker, D.J. *Spanish Women and the Colonial Wars.* Baton Rouge: Louisiana State University Press, May 2008.

Willbanks, James H. ed. *Generals of the Army: Marshall, MacArthur, Eisenhower, Arnold, Bradley*. Lexington: University of Kentucky Press, 2013.

Wynn, Neil A. *Historical Dictionary from the Great War to the Great Depression*. Lanham: Scarecrow Press, 2014.

Yoshiaki, Yoshimi. *Comfort Women: Sexual Slavery in the Japanese Military During World War II*. New York: Columbia University Press, 1995.

Journal Articles

Lanzona, Vina A. "Capturing the Huk Amazons: Representing Women Warriors in the Philippines, 1940s-1950s." *South East Asia Research*, Vol. 17 No. 2 (July 2009): 133-174.

Sergeant Karl Ritt. "Filipino Nurses on Bataan." *American Journal of Nursing*, Vol. 45 No. 5 (May 1945): 346-347.

Government Sources

The U.S. National Archives and Records Administration. "Military Records: Guerrilla Units." *The Philippine Archives Collection*.
https://www.archives.gov/research/military/ww2/philippine/guerrilla-list-1.html.

The U.S. National Archives and Records Administration. "Guerrilla Unit Recognition Files, 1941-1948." *The Philippine Archives Collection*.
https://catalog.archives.gov/id/1257644.

U.S. Department of Veterans Affairs. WWII Filipino Veterans Equity Compensation (FVEC) Fund." *Center for*

Minority Veterans. Last Modified April 11th, 2018.
https://www.va.gov/centerforminorityveterans/fvec.asp.

Theses

Larry S. Schmidt. *American Involvement in the Filipino Resistance Movement on Mindanao During the Japanese Occupation, 1942-1945, Master of Military Art and Science Thesis.* U.S. Army Command and General Staff College, 1982.

News & Internet Resources

ABS-CBN News Correspondent. "Last Hukbalahap Commander Dies, Age 92." *ABS-CBN.Com.* Last Modified July 3, 2015. Last Accessed August 17th, 2018.
http://news.abs-cbn.com/nation/regions/07/02/15/last-hukbalahap-commander-dies-age-92.

Arcellaz, Princess Clea. "San Simon Pays Tribute to Kumander Guerrero." *Sun Star Philippines.* Last Modified July 5th, 2015. Last Accessed August 17th, 2018.
https://www.sunstar.com.ph/article/18277/.

Bartolome, Jessica. "Kumander Guerrero will Live On: Remembering Simeona Tapang." Last Modified July 7th, 2015. Last Accessed August 17th, 2018.
http://www.gmanetwork.com/news/lifestyle/content/517646/kumander-guerrero-will-live-on-remembering-simeona-tapang/story/.

Caballes, "10 Kickass Pilipina Warriors that You Probably Never Heard of," *Pinoy Culture.com: Your Source for Everything Pilipino,* Last Modified August 28th, 2014,

Last Accessed August 23rd, 2018.
http://pinoy-culture.com/10-kickass-pilipina-warriors-in-history-that-you-probably-never-heard-of/.

Cabico, Gaea Katreena. "Gabriela Solons Seek Probe Into Removal of Comfort Woman Statue." *PhilStar News*, Last Modified May 10th, 2018. Last Accessed December 28th, 2018.
https://www.philstar.com/headlines/2018/05/10/1813942/gabriela-solons-seek-probe-removal-comfort-woman-statue.

Celdran, Beatrice. "I Am... Woman: Historic Filipinas." *Philippine Tatler*. Last Modified August 7th, 2014. Last Accessed August 23rd, 2018.
https://ph.asiatatler.com/life/i-am-woman.

Xiao Chua. "'Lioness of PHL guerilla spies' Maggie Leones To Be Buried With Full Honors." *GMA News Online*. Last Modified June 11th, 2016. Last Accessed December 27th, 2018.
https://www.gmanetwork.com/news/lifestyle/content/573214/lioness-of-phl-guerilla-spies-maggie-leones-to-be-buried-with-full-honors/story/.

Chua, Xiao. "JOSEFA LLANES ESCODA AT ANG MGA PASAWAY NA BABAE NOONG DIGMAAN." *It's Xiao Time!* Last Modified January 31st, 2013. Last Accessed August 17th, 2018.
https://xiaochua.net/2013/01/31/xiaotime-31-january-2013-josefa-llanes-escoda-at-ang-mga-pasaway-na-babae-noong-digmaan/.

Dietz, Lorna. "The Story of a Rare and Great Hero." *SCRIBD*. Las Modified December 2011. Last Accessed August 17th, 2018.
https://www.scribd.com/document/75503075/Lourdes-

Castro-1926-2011-The-Story-of-a-Rare-and-Great-Hero.

FilipiKnow.net. "The 10 Most Incredible Filipina Warriors of World War II." *FilipiKnow*. Last Modified 2018, Last Accessed December 17th, 2018. https://filipiknow.net/filipina-heroes-of-wwii/#2_Elena_Poblete.

GMA News. "Last Living Huk Commander Passes Away a Day Before Her 93rd Birthday." *GMA News Online*. Last Modified July 2, 2015. Last Accessed December 18th, 2018. https://www.gmanetwork.com/news/lifestyle/content/514518/last-living-huk-commander-passes-away-a-day-before-93rd-birthday/story/.

Guillermo, Emil. "Magdalena Leones, Filipina World War II Silver Star Recipient Who Aided MacArthur, Dies in California." Last Modified July 5th, 2016. Last Accessed August 17th, 2018. https://www.nbcnews.com/news/asian-america/magdalena-leones-filipina-wwii-silver-star-recepient-who-aided-macarthur-n603566.

IMDB. "American Guerrilla In the Philippines." *IMDB.Com*. https://www.imdb.com/title/tt0042195/?ref_=ttfc_fc_tt.

Jayme, Tessie. "Red Cross in Manila." *Black Clouds in Manila*. Last Modified March 1st, 2014. Last Accessed August 17th, 2018. http://blackcloudsinmanila.com/Home.php.

De Leon, Dwight. "WWII Filipina Spy Dies at 95." *Rappler News, Philippines*. Last Modified June 24th, 2016. Last Accessed August 17th, 2018. https://www.rappler.com/move-ph/137362-world-war-filipina-spy-magdalena-leones.

Maceda, Marichu. "Carmen Rosales: The Genuine Super-
    star." *PhilStar Global*. Last Modified March 6th, 2005.
    Last Accessed December 27th, 2018.
    https://www.philstar.com/entertainment/2005/03/06/
    269261/carmen-rosales-genuine-superstar.

Orejas, Tonette. "Pension Elusive for Aeta Guerrillas." *In-
    quirer.Net*. Last Modified March 2nd, 2014. Last Ac-
    cessed December 28th, 2018.
    https://newsinfo.inquirer.net/769917/pension-elusive-
    for-aeta-guerrillas.

Orejas, Tonette. "Liwayway: Warrior Who Wore Lipstick in
    Gun Battles." *Inquirer.Net Central Luzon*. Last Modified
    May 17th, 2014. Last Accessed August 17th, 2018.
    https://newsinfo.inquirer.net/602758/liwayway-warrior-
    who-wore-lipstick-in-gun-battles.

Osaki, Tomohiro. "Abe Rejects Seoul's New Call for Apology
    On 'Comfort Women' Issue." *Japan Times*. Last Modified
    January 12th, 2018. Last Accesed December 21st, 2018.
    https://www.japantimes.co.jp/news/2018/01/12/national
    /politics-diplomacy/abe-rejects-kangs-new-apology-
    call-comfort-women-issue/.

Palafox, Quennie Ann J. "Lest We Forget our Unsung
    Founding Mothers." *Inquirer.Net*. Last Last Modified
    June 12th, 2011. Accessed August 17th, 2018.
    http://newsinfo.inquirer.net/14134/lest-we-forget-our-
    unsung-founding-mothers.

Pre-Medical Society of the Ateneo. "Filipina Angels of Ba-
    taan." *The Pre-Medical Society of the Ateneo*. Last Modi-
    fied April 9th, 2015. Last Accessed December 27th, 2018.
    https://www.facebook.com/the.pmsa/photos/a.14652874
    2097296/810066542410176/?type=1&theater.

Rare Historical Photos. "Captain Nieves Fernandez Shows to an American Soldier how She Used her Long Knife to Silently Kill Japanese Soldiers During Occupation, 1944." *RareHistoricalPhotos.Com.* Last Modified June 21st, 2014. Last Accessed August 17th, 2018. https://rarehistoricalphotos.com/captain-nieves-fernandez-1944/.

Richardson, Jim. "Celia Mariano Pomeroy: Communist Revolutionary Who Went on to Teach in London Primary Schools." *Independent Minds.* Last Modified October 22, 2009, Last Accessed December 18th, 2018. https://www.independent.co.uk/news/obituaries/celia-mariano-pomeroy-communist-revolutionary-who-went-on-to-teach-in-london-primary-schools-1806786.html.

Sellers, Michael. "Captain Nieves Fernandez – WWII Guerrilla Leader in Leyte, Philippines." *Michael Sellers.com.* Last Modified February 11th, 2017. Last Accessed August 15th, 2018. http://www.michaeldsellers.com/blog/2017/02/11/looking-for-info-on-captain-nieves-fernandez-wwii-guerrilla-leader-in-leyte-philippines/.

Snafu, Doc. "(USAFFE) (Far East) Guerrilla Movement, Philippines, 1942-1945." *EUCMH Exposition Blog.* Last Modified July 17th, 2015. Last Accessed August 15th, 2018. https://www.eucmh.com/2015/07/17/usaffe-far-east-guerrilla-movement-philippines-1942-1945/.

Tantingco, Robby. "Why Women Rule Pampanga." *Positively Filipino: Your Window on the Filipino Diaspora.* Last Modified March 10th, 2015. Last Accessed August 17th, 2018.

http://www.positivelyfilipino.com/magazine/why-women-rule-pampanga.

Templo, Mike. "Claiming Veterans' Benefits Under Obama's Stimulus Package-Atty. Mike Templo." Last Modified February 28th, 2009. Last Accessed August 20th, 2018. http://news.abs-cbn.com/views-and-analysis/02/27/09/claiming-veterans-benefits-under-obamas-stimulus-package-atty-mike-templ.

Unknown Author. "School Ma'am Led Guerrillas On Leyte." *Lewiston Daily Sun*, October 26th, 1944. Last Accessed August 15th, 2018. http://www.michaeldsellers.com/blog/2017/02/11/looking-for-info-on-captain-nieves-fernandez-wwii-guerrilla-leader-in-leyte-philippines/.

Video 48. "Carmen Rosales." *Video 48: A Virtual Online Library and Archive On Philippine Cinema*. Last Modified April 30th 2008. Last Accessed December 27th, 2018. http://video48.blogspot.com/search?q=Carmen+Rosales.

Video 48, "THE FIFTIES # 618: PANCHO MAGALONA AND ROSA ROSAL IN LAMBERTO V. AVELLANA'S "CRY FREEDOM" (1959)," *Video48: A Virtual Online Library and Archive of Philippine Cinema*, Last Modified April 22nd, 2014, Last Accessed December 27h, 2018. http://video48.blogspot.com/2014/04/the-fifties-618-pancho-magalona-and.html.

Watawat.net. "The Wha-Chi and Other Guerrilla Groups and Units." *Watawat: Flags and Symbols of the Pearl of the Orient Seas*, Last Modified 2017. Last Accessed December 17th, 2018. http://www.watawat.net/the-wha-chi--and-other-guerrilla-groups-and-units.html.

Welteke, Karl. "Corregidor-Then and Now: 503rd PRCT Heritage Battalion, The Fall of the Philippines, Battle of Manila." *Corregidorproboards.com*, Last Modified August 3rd, 2015. Last Accessed December 22nd, 2018. http://corregidor.proboards.com/thread/1848/general-wainwright.

Yoder, Robert L. "Philippine Heroines of the Revolution: Maria Clara They Were Not." *Austrian-Philippine*. Last Modified September 1, 1999. Last Accessed August 17th, 2018. https://www.univie.ac.at/ksa/apsis/aufi/wstat/heroine.htm.

Archives, Oral Histories, & Personal Collections

Aremas, Sherry. (World War II Philippine Guerrilla, Salinas *manang* pre-1965 generation), interviewed by Stacey Salinas. April 2018.

Aremas, Susan. (Bridge Generation Filipina American, primary school teacher, daughter of the *manong* generation), interviewed by Stacey Salinas. January – April 2018.

Congressional Record. *United States of America: Congressional Record: Proceedings and Debates of the 111th Congress, First Session*. Washington: United States Government Printing Office, 2009.

Danny Dolor. "Carmen Rosales as Guerilyera." Last Modified June 14th, 2014. Last Accessed December 27th, 2018. https://www.pressreader.com/philippines/the-philippine-star/20150614/282402693010462.

Dec, Billy. "Honoring Filipino WWII Veterans this Filipino American History Month." *The White House: President Barack Obama*. Last Modified October 3rd, 2016. Last

Accessed December 24th, 2018.
https://obamawhitehouse.archives.gov/blog/2016/10/03/
honoring-filipino-wwii-veterans-filipino-american-
history-month.

The Philippines Mail. Microfilm. John Steinbeck Public Library, Salinas, California.

Photographs. Aremas Family Personal Collection. Salinas, California.

Poblete, Lourdes. (World War II Guerrilla, Filipina American medical worker), interviewed by Stacey Salinas. June 2017.

The U.S. National Archives and Records Administration. "Military Records: Guerrilla Units." *The Philippine Archives Collection.*
https://www.archives.gov/research/military/ww2/philippine/guerrilla-list-1.html.

The U.S. National Archives and Records Administration. "Guerrilla Unit Recognition Files, 1941-1948." *The Philippine Archives Collection.*
https://catalog.archives.gov/id/1257644.

The U.S. National Archives and Records Administration. "Department of Defense. Far East Command. Philippines Command. Guerrilla Affairs Division. 8/1/1948-10/14/1949." Series: Records Relating to the U.S. Army Recognition Program of Philippine Guerrillas, ca. 1949 – ca. 1949 Record Group 554: Records of General Headquarters, Far East Command, Supreme Commander Allied Powers, and United Nations Command, 1945-1960. https://catalog.archives.gov/id/6921767.

U.S. Citizenship and Immigration Services. "USCIS to Implement Filipino World War II Veterans Parole Program. *USCIS.* Last Modified May 9th, 2016. Last Accessed December 24th, 2018.

https://www.uscis.gov/news/news-releases/uscis-implement-filipino-world-war-ii-veterans-parole-program.

Westpoint. "Guerrillas in the Philippines." *West-Point.org*. http://www.west-point.org/family/japanese-pow/Guerrillas/Guerrillas-Main.htm.

Films

Magalona, Pancho & Rosa Rosal. *Cry Freedom*. Directed by Lamberto V. Avellana. Parallel Film Distribution, Inc., Metro Manila, 1959.

Power, Tyrone & Micheline Presle. *American Guerrilla In the Philippines* 1950. Directed by Fritz Lang. 20th Century Fox, 1950.

De La Rosa, Rogelio & Norma Blancaflor. *Victory Joe*. Directed by Manuel Silos. LVN Pictures, Metro Manila, 1946.

Rosales, Carmen & Jaime De La Rosa. *Batalyon XIII*. Directed by Manuel Silos. LVN Pictures, Metro Manila, 1949.

Rosales, Carmen & Tita Dura. *Guerilyera*. Directed by Octavio Silos. Sampaguita Pictures, 1946.

Made in the USA
Middletown, DE
25 September 2021

49044440R00102